国际商务函电

Business Communication

主　编　**邓来英　刘　芬**
副主编　**杨晓青**
编　者　**曹诗娴　马菲菲**

清华大学出版社
北　京

内 容 简 介

　　本教材以培养商务英语专业学生的英语书面表达和沟通能力为目标，以外贸企业典型业务工作流程为主线展开编写。教材共11章，涵盖商务函电基础知识和外贸业务的各环节，包括建立业务联系、询盘、报盘和还盘、接受与订单、签订合同、支付、包装、保险、运输、投诉与索赔等。每个章节都以任务为导向，包含导学、外贸知识、信函样例、情景对话和拓展阅读等部分，并专门列出了函电撰写功能句型，精心设计了业务技能训练。业务技能训练中还有各类习题和信函撰写练习，旨在从不同角度淬炼学生的商务知识和函电撰写沟通技能，使学生能够将商务知识和语言技能融会贯通，为将来走向商务类岗位打下坚实的基础。教材配有电子课件、微课视频和练习参考答案，读者可从www.tsinghuaelt.com下载使用。

　　本书既可作为普通高等院校商务英语、国际贸易及相关专业的教材，也可作为外贸从业人员的参考用书，还可作为外贸培训行业的培训辅导用书。

图书在版编目（CIP）数据

国际商务函电：英文 / 邓来英，刘芬主编. —北京：清华大学出版社，2023.1（2023.8重印）
ISBN 978-7-302-62490-5

Ⅰ. ①国…　Ⅱ. ①邓…　②刘…　Ⅲ. ①国际商务—英语—电报信函—写作—高等职业教育—教材
Ⅳ. ① F740

中国国家版本馆 CIP 数据核字（2023）第 005101 号

责任编辑：刘　艳
封面设计：子　一
责任校对：王凤芝
责任印制：刘海龙

出版发行：清华大学出版社
　　　　网　　　址：http://www.tup.com.cn, http://www.wqbook.com
　　　　地　　　址：北京清华大学学研大厦 A 座　　　　　　邮　　编：100084
　　　　社 总 机：010-83470000　　　　　　　　　　　　　邮　　购：010-62786544
　　　　投稿与读者服务：010-62776969, c-service@tup.tsinghua.edu.cn
　　　　质量反馈：010-62772015, zhiliang@tup.tsinghua.edu.cn
印 装 者：三河市天利华印刷装订有限公司
经　　销：全国新华书店
开　　本：185mm×260mm　　　　　印　　张：14.5　　　　　字　　数：309 千字
版　　次：2023 年 1 月第 1 版　　　　　印　　次：2023 年 8 月第 2 次印刷
定　　价：59.00 元

产品编号：098739-01

前　言

近年来，在"互联网+"政策的影响下，我国的外贸规模持续扩大。同时，除了传统外贸之外，跨境电商也得到了迅猛发展。日新月异的外贸新形势要求高校培养出具有语言能力、商务能力、跨文化交流能力的复合型、应用型、创新型商务人才。在此背景下，为帮助学生掌握外贸函电知识，并能在实际工作中灵活娴熟地运用，编者走访数家外贸企业，听取了多名企业专家意见，并结合多年工作经验编写了《国际商务函电》一书。

一、教材特色

《国际商务函电》主要以培养商务英语专业学生的英语书面表达和沟通能力为目标，以外贸企业典型业务工作流程为主线展开编写，将外贸知识与商务英语语言能力有机结合起来，为学生将来从事外贸工作，运用函电有效进行业务联络和沟通奠定坚实的基础。其特色主要有：

- 内容丰富。本教材紧密结合行业标准，遵循学生的认知发展规律，不仅简述了惯用的商务英语信函，还介绍了相关外贸知识，总结了每个主题的重点功能句型，列举了典型场景对话等，帮助学生熟练掌握外贸流程及其往来函电的撰写规范及沟通要点。

- 实践性强。本教材以任务为导向，教学合一，突出实践性；每个单元的设计从导入到拓展阅读部分都围绕同一个特定的商务主题，以任务为主线展开，从不同角度使学生得以举一反三地淬炼商务知识和函电撰写沟通技能，融"教、学、做"为一体，充分发挥学生的主体作用，通过"做中学""做中教""学中悟"实现教学目标，全面提升学生的商务英语沟通技能。

二、内容体例

《国际商务函电》共包含 11 个单元，除第一单元为总体介绍外，每个单元包括以下 6 个部分：

- 外贸知识（Business Knowledge）。两篇与主题密切相关的外贸知识阅读文章能帮助学生快速了解外贸进出口业务各环节涉及的专业知识和专业术语，增强外贸知识储备，提升英语沟通能力。

- 信函学习（Case Study）。四篇典型商务信函能让学生习得各主题信函要点和信函撰写技巧，并能根据不同的情境撰写布局得当、措辞得体、内容贴切、格式正确的往来信函。

- 功能句型（Functional Sentence Patterns）。常用表达句式的总结将进一步巩固学生的语言技能，使学生能够实现从商务信函的输入到交际输出的能力提升。

- 情景对话（Situational Dialogs）。情景对话示范及角色扮演可使学生在情境中熟悉商务主题活动、常见的语言表达等，巩固所学的商务知识和语言表达，提升商务沟通技能，满足就业上岗的需要。

- 技能训练（Skill Training）。课后丰富多样的习题训练可帮助学生检验学习效果，深化对知识的理解，并进一步内化为商务知识和商务交际能力。

- 拓展阅读（Additional Reading）。该部分旨在拓宽学生的国际视野，加深对相关主题的理解并培养其自主学习能力。

本教材由邓来英、刘芬担任主编，杨晓青担任副主编，曹诗娴、马菲菲参加编写，最后由邓来英、刘芬、杨晓青负责全书的统稿、定稿工作。在编写过程中，本教材得到了广州市信川电子商务有限公司的江拓先生和广州博文礼品贸易公司的袁方女士的鼎力支持，他们为本教材的编写提供了大量外贸业务信函，在此表示诚挚的感谢。

本教材可供商务英语、国际贸易及相关专业的学生使用，也可供广大从事国际商贸工作、希望提高商务沟通能力的人士使用。教材配有电子课件、微课视频和练习参考答案，能更好地满足各类学习者的需要，读者可从 www.tsinghuaelt.com 下载使用。

由于时间仓促，书中不妥之处在所难免，恳请广大读者批评指正。

编者

2022 年 10 月

Contents

Chapter 1
Fundamentals of Business Communication 1

Chapter 2
Establishment of Business Relations 21

Chapter 3
Enquiry 43

Chapter 4
Offer and Counter Offer 61

Chapter 5
Acceptance and Orders..................................81

Chapter 6
Contracts 99

Chapter 7
Payment 119

Chapter 8
Packing 141

Chapter 9
Insurance... 163

Chapter 10
Shipment 181

Chapter 11
Complaints and Claims 201

Chapter 12

Chapter 1

Fundamentals of Business Communication

Learning Objectives

By completing this unit, students will learn:

- the basic parts of a business English letter;
- the writing principles of business English letters;
- the formats of business English letters;
- the email etiquette.

Lead-in

Work in groups, discuss the following questions and then share your answers with the whole class.

1. What are the differences between Chinese letter writing and English letter writing?

2. What are the parts of a business letter?

3. Does business writing play an important role in business communication? Why or why not?

4. What are the principles and formats of business writing?

5. What is email etiquette?

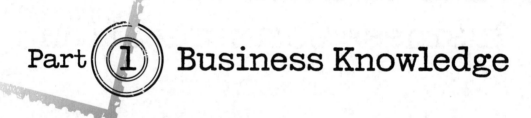

Part ① Business Knowledge

Section 1 | Basic Parts of a Business English Letter

Generally speaking, a business letter is made up of seven essential parts: letterhead, date, inside name and address, salutation, body, complimentary close, and signature. Under some circumstances, six optional parts may also be contained, namely attention line, subject line/caption, reference notation, enclosure, carbon copy and postscript. Here is the detailed introduction of the seven essential parts.

Letterhead

The letterhead expresses a firm's personality and is generally printed on the firm's stationery. It helps to form the impression of the writer's firm. Styles vary considerably, but they all give similar information, and usually include all or some of the following elements: the company's name and address, postcode, telephone number, fax number, email address, and even website. They are usually positioned in the center of the top.

Date

Business letters should have the correct date typed under the letterhead. The date should be typed or written in full form rather than in abbreviated form, since the date records when the letter is written and may serve as an important reference. Usually, the date is shown in the order of day/month/ year (British practice), or month/day/year (American practice).

Pay attention to the following points about the date line:

- Year should be typed in full. Avoid abbreviations. For example, 2022 cannot be replaced by 22.
- Month is preferably spelled out in letters, to avoid confusion. For example, 12/11 can be November 12 or December 11.
- Day can be written either in cardinal numbers or ordinal numbers. Hence, the recommended forms for the date are as follows: October 25, 2022 or October 25th, 2022.

Inside Name and Address

This part consists of the name and complete address of the receiver. Although the address already appears on the envelope, you should still put the inside name and address in the letter because the envelope is usually thrown away. Then the letter itself, which is to be kept on file, can indicate to whom the message is addressed. It is usually placed two lines below the date line, aligned with the left margin.

If the letter is addressed to a group, the inside address includes only the address and the group name. If it is to a person, use either a courtesy title or a professional title. Care should be taken to address the recipient as exactly as it appears on the envelope of the letter.

Salutation

Salutation is a complimentary greeting with which every letter begins. Salutation can be followed by a comma or a colon. Colon is formal in American business letters, comma in British ones. Be sure to salute to the correct addressee appearing in your inside address or in the attention line.

The customary formal greeting in a business letter is "Dear Sir(s) / Dear Madam(s)," or an official title like "President/Doctor". If the receiver is known to the writer personally, a less formal and warmer greeting is used: "Dear Mr. Johnson / Dear Ms. Fanon".

Body

Body is the most important part of a letter since it contains the actual message. The body of the letter deserves special attention no matter how brief it may be. Careful planning and logical arrangement are needed for the paragraphs. A typical three-paragraph letter would be like the following:

- The opening paragraph should be short, probably no more than two or three lines, and easy to understand.

- The middle paragraph supports the first paragraph and provides more information. Here, try to bring in your involvement, for example, what your purpose of writing the letter is, or what service or information you can offer.

- The closing paragraph is the summary of the letter; it stresses the action that you want the reader to take and you should keep the closing short and friendly.

Complimentary Close

The complimentary close is simply a polite way to end a letter. The expression for the complimentary close should match the salutation. It appears in the middle of the page and two lines below the closing sentence for indented layout while it starts at the left-hand margin for fully blocked letters. Only the initial letter in the first word of any complimentary close is capitalized.

Signature

The signature is the signed name or seal of the writer. It is generally put two lines below the complimentary close and should be signed by hand and in ink. Under the handwritten signature, the signer's name and his or her position are usually followed in typing.

Exercises

I. **Decide whether the statements are true (T) or false (F) according to the passage.**

1. Generally speaking, a business letter consists of seven essential parts and six optional parts. (   )

2. The letterhead helps to form the impression of the writer's firm, which usually includes the company's name and contact information. (   )

3. 9/11, 2022 is a right way to show the date. (   )

4. Inside name and address can be left out since they already appear on the envelope. (   )

5. Body is the most important part of a letter, which is made up of three paragraphs. (   )

6. Signature should be signed both by hand and in ink. Sometimes the signer's name and his or her position are followed under the handwritten signature. (   )

II. **Read the given letter carefully, and find out each component of a business letter. The first one has been done for your reference.**

1. Guangzhou Lulin Textile Import and Export Corp.

207 Guangyuan Road

Guangzhou 510000, China

Telephone: 020–34118336

Fax: 020–34118336

Email: Lulin@hotmail.com.cn

2. 25th December, 2022

3. Herry Trading Co. Ltd.

Akeksanterink Street

P. O. BOX 9, FINLAND

Attention: Purchasing Dept.

4. Dear Sirs,

5. Thank you for your offer of December 5th.

Because of the keen competition in the market, we regret to inform you that we cannot accept your quotation. It would leave us only a small profit. Actually, we are receiving an off er from another seller, and their price is 10% lower than that of yours. In view of our long friendly business relationship, we suggest that you reduce your price at least by 8%.

We are looking forward to your favorable reply.

6. Yours truly,

7. Wennie

8.   Reference Notation

9.   Enclosures

10. Cc: our Beijing Branch Office

11. P.S. Can I have your Skype?

1.   letterhead   2. _____

3. _____   4. _____

5. _____   6. _____

7. _____   8. _____

9. _____   10. _____

11. _____

Section 2 Writing Principles of Business English Letters

Business English letters play an important role in the development of goodwill and friendly trade relationships. They should be friendly and courteous, easy to read and easy to understand. In writing a business letter, there are generally seven principles for you to follow, namely 7Cs.

Courtesy

Be as polite as possible. It can set up an honest and enthusiastic image in the eyes of the readers who will be glad to cooperate with you. Therefore, you should not only use some phrases like "please" or "thank you", but also keep a sincere you-attitude and try to avoid irritating, offensive, or belittling statements even when you do have to blame your receivers.

Clarity

It means your purpose and words are clear to your readers so that they will not misunderstand what you are trying to convey. Be certain about what you wish to say, express it in plain, simple words, and present it in well-constructed sentences and paragraphs. For example, use "never" instead of "under no circumstances"; use "as requested" instead of "as per your request".

Conciseness

It means to clearly express what you would do in a short and pithy style of writing without sacrificing completeness and courtesy. Sometimes repetition is necessary for emphasis. But if the same thing is said several times without reason, the business English letter will be boring. For example, "Will you ship us any time during the month of November, or even December if you are rushed, for December would suit us just as well?" In this sentence, what the writer wants to express is that the reader can ship the goods during November/December, so you can put the sentence into "Please make shipment during November/December". That will be enough to clearly express the writer's intention, and there is no need to repeat.

Consideration

It means you prepare the writing with the reader in mind and try to put yourself in his or her place. You should focus on "you" instead of "I" and "we", trying to give consideration to the receivers' wishes, demands, interests and difficulties by adopting their viewpoints. Moreover, use positive sentences instead of negative sentences, since negative sentences tend to sound critical of the reader and disappointed on the part of the writer, while positive sentences sound encouraging to both parties. It would serve the function of effective communication if you sometimes turn negative messages into positive ones.

Completeness

It means to contain all facts that the receiver needs and desires. Business English letters are complete when they contain all the necessary information. The letter should never leave questions previously prompted by the reader unanswered. Hence, you should make all points detailed and answer all questions asked.

Concreteness

Be sure to be specific, definite and convincing, rather than vague, general and abstract, or the reader will be at a loss, and don't know what you are talking about. For example, "We regret to note that your client wants to cancel his order" is not specific, and if it is changed into "We regret to note that your client wants to cancel his order for textiles", it would be much better.

Correctness

It refers to not only appropriate and grammatically correct language, but also reliable information and accurate figures (such as name of article, specification, quantity, price, etc.).

I. **Match the words in the left column with their translations in the middle column and definitions in the right column.**

1. courtesy   A. 具体   a. the fact of containing all the necessary information and answering all the questions put forward by the readers

2. clarity   B. 体谅   b. the correct usage of grammar, punctuation, spelling, standard language, and proper statements

3. conciseness   C. 完整   c. polite behavior that shows respect for other people

4. consideration   D. 正确   d. the quality of being specific, definite, and persuasive

5. completeness   E. 清楚   e. the fact of being short and pithy, with no unnecessary words

6. concreteness   F. 简洁   f. the quality of being expressed clearly

7. correctness   G. 礼貌   g. the quality of thinking about other people's feelings and being careful not to upset them

II. **Read the passage and answer the following questions.**

1. How important are business English letters?

_____

2. Why should you be courteous when writing business English letters?

_____

3. How can you achieve the effect of clarity when writing business English letters?

_____

4. What are the differences between courtesy and consideration?

_____

5. Why are positive sentences more effective than negative sentences?

_____

Section 3 Formats of Business English Letters

The main aim of designing a letter is to make it not only pleasing to the eye, but also convenient to be typed. Basically, there are mainly four styles of business letters—the conventional indented style, the modern blocked style, the modified style, and the simplified style, among which, the first two are the most widely used. Whichever form is employed, a common business English letter consists of seven essential parts. Sometimes the letter might contain some or all the optional parts.

In the indented style, the first line of each paragraph is indented, the subject line is put in the center, and the complimentary close and signature are put on the right. Moreover, each line in the letterhead and the inside name and address is indented one or two spaces.

In the blocked style, all parts of the letter begin from the left margin and paragraphs are not indented. It is convenient to be typed with a typewriter but the layout is not so beautiful.

The modified style is the mixture of the above two formats, which is more suitable for friends or people with close relationship. In the modified style, some parts remain blocked with the body paragraphs, allowing some other parts—both essential and optional parts—indented.

In the simplified style, all parts of a letter begin from the left margin, but it leaves out the salutation and the complimentary close.

Exercises

I. Decide whether the statements are true (T) or false (F) according to the passage.

1. A letter should be designed to be eye-pleasing and convenient to be typed. (   )

2. Whichever style is applied, a common business English letter consists of seven essential parts. (   )

3. The most beautiful layout is the blocked style. (   )

4. In the indented style, the first line of each paragraph is not indented. (   )

5. The modified style is the mixture of the blocked style and the indented style. (   )

6. The simplified form is somewhat like the blocked form. But some parts are omitted. (   )

II. Read the following letters and decide which format each letter belongs to.

Letter 1: _____

Mail box No. 82

GD University

Guangzhou, Guangdong, China

Dec. 18th, 2022

Pigeon Hotel

Linggong Road 1818

Beijing, China

Dear Sir/Madam,

I'm writing in response to your advertisement for establishing business relations. I would like to express my sincere hope to establish business relations with you.

I am sending you the quotation sheet and brochures for your information, and look forward to hearing from you.

Yours faithfully,

William Jerry

Letter 2: _____

Ken's Cheese House

34 Chatley Avenue, Seattle, WA 98765

Fax: 010–1234569, Email: kenny@cheese.com

Nov. 20th, 2022

William & Jones

67 Guts Road

Oxford, OX4 2JR, UK

Dear Sirs,

Thank you for your enquiry in your letter of Nov. 12th...

We hope to hear from you soon.

Yours faithfully,

Gary Johnson

Section 4 Email Etiquette

As communication continues to evolve to be almost entirely electronic, it would be a good time to provide a few reminder points about communicating via email effectively, both internally with colleagues and externally with guests and clients. Email is sometimes the only medium by which we have relationship with guests and clients and it is by far the most frequent means of communication we use. Please keep in mind that everything intended for internal use could easily find its way to external communication, so the same thoughts should apply.

A sending-out email generally consists of the following parts: the receiver, carbon copy or blind carbon copy, subject, attachment, and body. In addition to familiarizing yourself with the interface of emails, you should also keep the following guidelines in mind.

- Keep emails short and to the point—send a more effective message by avoiding misunderstandings and inappropriate comments; don't send emails that are too long; try to keep your sentences to a maximum of 15 to 20 words.

- Write the action you are requesting and topic in the "subject" line—ensure that you have a relevant subject, describing what you need clearly in the subject line.

- Check grammar and spelling. If second language support, like English, is required, ask a colleague to review the email before sending. Emails should never be sent with spelling or grammatical errors, especially to guests and clients.

- Formality is in place as a courtesy and reflects respect. Be courteous, considerate, and responsible when writing an email—communication via email is often considered informal, but you shouldn't treat it that way.

- Open an email with a polite salutation like "Dear..." and end with a complimentary close, such as "Thank you", "Sincerely", "Best regards", etc.

- Do not type in all capital letters. If you write in capitals, it seems as if you are shouting. This can be highly annoying and might trigger an unwanted response in the form of a flame email.

- When making points, number them or mark each point as separate to keep the overall view clear.

- If your email address is a business address, be sure to include your title and company name in the signature.

- Think before you send an email—once an email is sent, it is gone. Think "Would you want the whole world to see this?" before you send it.

While most of these points are well known to you, an occasional reminder can help to keep the key points top of mind.

Exercises

I. **Read the passage and choose the best answer to each question.**

1. Regarding communicating via email, _____.

   A. it is always the only way that we contact our clients

   B. it is not worthy of being reminded

   C. it is not effective when we contact our colleagues

   D. email etiquette for internal use also applies to external use

2. A sending-out email is generally made up of the following parts EXCEPT _____.

   A. the receiver

   B. carbon copy or blind carbon copy

   C. inside name and address

   D. subject, attachment, and body

3. On keeping email short and to the point, which of the following statements is NOT true?

   A. Use more abbreviations.

   B. Don't use words that easily cause misunderstanding.

   C. Don't send emails with long paragraphs.

   D. Don't use unsuitable comments.

4. Why shouldn't you write an email in all capitals?

   A. It is illegible.   B. It is informal.

   C. It is annoying.   D. It is unsuitable.

5. Which of the following statements is NOT true?

   A. There is no need for you to be courteous and considerate, since emails are informal ways of communication.

   B. Use proper spelling and grammar when writing emails.

   C. It is better for you to number the points or mark each point in an email.

   D. Think twice before you send your email.

II. Recognize and write down the parts of a sending-out email interface. The first one has been done for your reference.

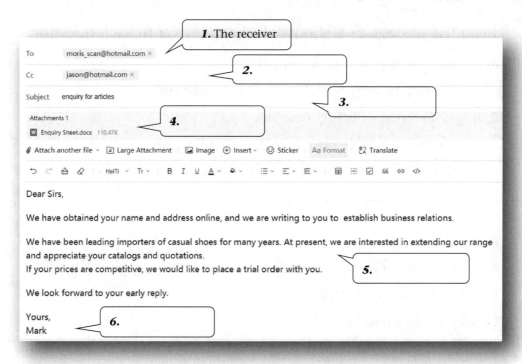

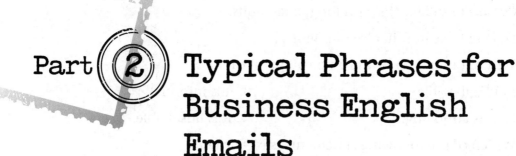

Part ② Typical Phrases for Business English Emails

1. **Making Reference**

    (1) About...

    (2) Following...

    (3) Thanks for your email...

2. **Replying to a Request**

    (1) As requested/suggested...

    (2) Here is/are...

    (3) As promised...

3. **Asking for Information or Advice**

    (1) Can you tell me about...

    (2) I'd like some information about...

    (3) I'd like your advice on...

4. **Attaching**

    (1) Please find attached a(n)...

    (2) Attached please find...

    (3) Attached is...

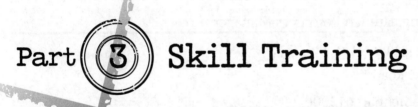

Part ③ Skill Training

I. **Arrange the following pieces of information in proper form as they should be set out in a letter in the blocked style.**

1. Sender's name: Royal Grosvenor Porcelain Company Ltd.

2. Sender's address: Grosvenor House, Renfrew Road, Oakley Staffordshire OA7 9DP

3. Date: Oct. 5th, 2022

4. Sender's telephone: (743069) 60621/4/8

5. Salutation: Dear Sirs,

6. Complimentary close: Yours truly,

7. Sender's telex: 70105 MAIEC

8. Body: Thank you for your letter of...

9. Sender's fax: (743069) 60621/4/8

10. Receiver's name: The Color Floor Co. Ltd.

11. Receiver's address: 126 Wilton Road, Axminister AXz AS

12. Attention line: Export Dept.

13. Subject line: Porcelain

14. Signature: Jimmy

II. Write a letter in the indented style, including the following paragraphs.

1. I would like to apologize for missing our scheduled appointment last Tuesday, Sept. 23rd, 2022. I also apologize for not calling in advance to cancel. I will call your office this week to reschedule a meeting with you.

2. Thank you for your understanding and patience.

3. From: Messers John Company Ltd.

   Celest Road, Demin, New York, 10043 NY, US

   Email: jmt@hotmail.com, Tel. 646–234876

4. To: James Tang, Human Resources Manager

   DAP Management Co. Ltd.

   56 Chunxi Road

   Chengdu, Sichuan 612000

III. Decide whether the following statements on the writing principles of business English letters are true (T) or false (F).

1. We should well plan the letter before starting to write. (   )

2. We can use difficult words and complicated structures to show that we are well educated. (   )

3. We'd better use some technical words to show that we are specialists in this field. (   )

4. Use scientific words as many as possible. (   )

5. Try to use short words. (   )

6. Delete words where possible. (   )

7. Avoid ordinary everyday English. (   )

IV. **Replace the following unfamiliar words with familiar ones.**

1. abbreviate _____   2. beverage _____

3. utilize _____   4. terminate _____

5. purchase _____   6. currently _____

7. modification _____   8. endeavor (*v.*) _____

9. subsequently _____   10. expenditure _____

V. **Improve the following sentences according to the 7Cs of writing business English letters and find out which principle each sentence breaks.**

1. You may encounter difficulties in terminating the contract.

2. I need your response immediately so that I can make the employee vacation schedule by next week.

3. There are two employees who should be promoted.

4. Will you ship us any time during the month of November, or even December if you are rushed, for December would suit us just as well?

5. This computer reproduces campaign letters fast.

VI. **Delete as many unnecessary words as possible in the following email to make it clear and complete.**

My dear Mr. Grayson,

I was informed earlier today by your colleague, Jane Rodder, that your company is now ready to consider our proposal. It goes without saying that I am delighted to hear this news. However, I will be on vacation in England for the next 5 days or so, and regrettably, during this period I will not be available to attend personally to any queries that you may have.

Notwithstanding the above, you will be telephoned by my secretary to arrange a little meeting after my return, when I hope this matter can be discussed further.

May I say that I very much look forward to meeting you?

With best wishes,

Brian Rodgers

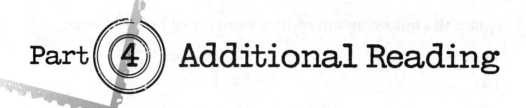

Part 4 Additional Reading

Email Etiquette when Representing Your Company

When sending emails on behalf of your company, whether you own it, run it or are an employee, you must always keep in mind that it's the company's image that stands to benefit or lose from the way you put that image out to the public, so there are a few helpful dos and don'ts.

Be Polite, Personal and On-Topic

First of all, when answering enquiries via email, always be polite, and try to somewhat personalize the message—by doing so, you will let the recipients understand that their query has actually been read and they're not being sent a standard company email. Be as concise as you can, as the enquiry is usually very specific, so that people looking for an answer won't have to hunt for it amidst irrelevant information.

The Time to Sell Is Not All the Time...

If you've been approached by potential customers with precise questions, a good idea would be not to pester them with every offer you can throw at them, as they might be put off altogether. Needless to say, great care must be taken to ensure their details are confidential and will not be used for other purposes, especially bombarding them with offers in the future, if they decide not to use your services after all.

If your company becomes known for aggressive marketing, it will definitely not help its reputation. As is the case with any kind of email, both the content and email address should remain confidential; the habit some companies have of exchanging email address lists is very much frowned upon.

Format Your Email with Care

Formatting is just as important as the content when you want to send a clear message. Using different fonts, colors, the bold, italic or underlined function or writing certain parts in capitals is likely to confuse the recipient, as it gives the impression that you want to stress the importance of those particular sentences or phrases. Thus, they might think you intend to class your statements by importance. It's advisable to use the same font and size, as well as not to overemphasize by using capitals, as some consider that to be the written equal of raising your voice.

Don't Sacrifice Grammar, Spelling or Punctuation to Speed

In terms of the time taken to reply, a prompt response, such as within 24 hours, demonstrates efficiency, as well as the fact that customer service is a priority. Before you send it, however, be sure to check the spelling and grammar, because if your email is deficient in that regard, your promptitude could be misinterpreted as haste to finish a formal task.

The correct use of punctuation is essential, since a formal email must never resemble a text message, where separating sentences is often disregarded. If a typo is overlooked, punctuation can completely change the meaning of a phrase as well as its tone. It's best that you keep sentences fairly short, in order to avoid generating confusion and boredom.

You Only Ever Get One Chance to Make a First Impression

Last but not least, as you stand for your company's interests and standards, remember to treat all customers or potential customers equally and especially leave them with the feeling that they've been treated respectfully. At first contact, never underestimate the importance an unknown individual could have for your business in the future.

Chapter 2

Establishment of Business Relations

Learning Objectives

By completing this unit, students will learn:

- ways to establish business relations and make credit status enquiries;
- how to analyze case letters on establishing business relations;
- useful expressions and sentence patterns related to establishing business relations;
- how to negotiate on establishing business relations.

Lead-in

Work in groups, discuss the following questions and then share your answers with the whole class.

1. Why does a company need extensive business connections?

2. Can you list some channels of obtaining business information?

3. What are the purposes of credit status enquiries? How can you make credit status enquiries?

4. What constituents should be included in a letter on establishing business relations?

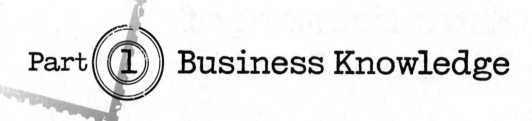

Part 1 Business Knowledge

Section 1 Ways to Establish Business Relations

Establishing business relations is the basis of starting and developing business. As the old saying goes, "No customers, no business." Modern business mostly depends on business relations. The more relations you build up, the more business you could have in hands. For instance, you can expand new markets deep into new fields of business activities. Therefore, it is vital to establish business relations with customers as extensively as possible.

In order to expand business, both the exporters and importers strive to find potential partners. Nowadays, a list of channels could be available for getting to know each other.

- Banks: They are always ready to supply the names and addresses of importers and exporters in their respective cities.

- Chambers of commerce: In almost every town or city of the world, there is a chamber of commerce, which is an organization of businessmen. One of its tasks is to collect business information and to find new business opportunities for members.

- Yellow pages: The world has rapidly transited into the digital age and with it, the way businesses around the world are now operating has also evolved. Yellow pages have continually bridged the gap between consumers and businesses for many years where businessmen can look for goods, services, directions and even deals all around the world.

- Official organizations: There are lots of official organizations in every country aiming at promoting economic development. These government organizations are happy to provide business opportunities to both importers and exporters at home and abroad.

- Trade fairs: A trade fair is an exhibition where companies in a specific industry can demonstrate their latest products, services, etc. There are great opportunities of getting business done in the fair, along with establishing business relations.

In addition, some other ways like advertisements, commercial counselor's offices, customs offices, hotline services, data banks, etc., are also useful for obtaining business information. They can help the exporters to find their partners and identify the markets they are going to penetrate or expand into.

What's more, there are also quite a few means of business communication such as telephone, telex, fax, email, e-commerce, and business letters. Often people enter into trade cooperation orally by telephone calls. Personal visits, face-to-face talks, discussions, and negotiations are also frequently used for the establishment of business relations.

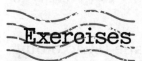

Exercises

I. **Read the passage and choose the best answer to each question.**

1. Which of the following statements is NOT the benefit of establishing business relations according to the passage?

A. Paving the way for future business.

B. Expanding new markets.

C. Entering into new business circles.

D. Consolidating business relations.

2. It can be concluded from the passage that the channels of establishing business relations are as follows EXCEPT _____.

A. trade fairs

B. chambers of commerce

C. import promotion organizations

D. banks

3. According to the passage, yellow pages _____.

A. have rapidly transited into the digital age

B. have helped companies to do business for a long time

C. only provide goods information and services for businessmen

D. will change the way of doing business in the future

4. As for the means of business communication, _____.

A. a variety of ways are widely used

B. people prefer to negotiate with each other by personal visits

C. people don't like writing letters to ask for establishing business relations

D. face-to-face talk is the most frequently used one

5. Which of the following statements is NOT true according to the passage?

A. Various ways can be applied to find potential business partners.

B. It is impossible to conclude transactions in the fair, but chances are great to establish business relations.

C. The exporters are eager to expand their business scopes.

D. Chambers of commerce are available in almost every town or city in the world.

II. **Decide whether the statements are true (T) or false (F) according to the passage.**

1. Nowadays, businessmen can choose various channels to obtain business information. (   )

2. Advertisements and trade fairs are not useful channels for obtaining business information. (   )

3. One can get business information from the chamber of commerce. (   )

4. Business communication can be conducted through telephone, telex, fax, email, e-commerce, and business letters effectively. (   )

Section 2 How to Make a Credit Status Enquiry

If you want to do business with a firm, you will have to know whether it is trustworthy. You will have to ask for credit information and must make sure you get paid for the products if you are an exporter. Therefore, making a credit status enquiry is of the utmost importance before a firm enters into real business relations with a new customer. Before a company makes a firm offer or plans to make an acceptance, it is advisable for its executive to make a credit status enquiry to avoid unnecessary risks of being cheated.

A credit status enquiry is to evaluate the current or potential customer's financial position and the ability to clear off his debts in order to decide the amount of credit to be granted to him. It is also called credit rating or credit standing. The function of a credit status enquiry is to get information concerning the financial position, credit (one's integrity in money matters and one's ability to meet payments when due), reputation, and business methods. Businessmen often speak of the 3Cs of credit, i.e., character, capacity, and capital. To obtain all the possible information respecting the firm one is about to enter into relations which will help to decide whether it is advisable to do business with the firm or not. It is a common practice for firms engaged in foreign trade to check out their possible new partners so as to avoid risks and financial losses. In international business, an exporter can turn to various ways for information as follows:

- Approaching firms that have supplied goods or services to the new company concerned;
- Contacting friends who have had business relations with the new customer for years;
- Applying to the trader's bank;
- Writing to relevant chambers of commerce.

Obviously, the information gained from the bank or from a chamber of commerce is generally the most reliable.

Moreover, when you are making status enquiries, it is necessary for them to be headed "Confidential" or "Private and Confidential" so that readers will pay special attention and care will be taken not to disclose their contents.

I. Read the passage and answer the following questions.

1. Why is it advisable for traders to make a credit status enquiry?

_____

2. What is credit rating or credit standing?

_____

3. What is the function of a status enquiry?

_____

4. What does 3Cs stand for?

_____

5. How do traders make a status enquiry? Which source is the most reliable?

_____

II. Match the words and phrases in the left column with their translations in the middle column and definitions in the right column.

1. bank reference   A. 商会   a. a statement showing the financial state of a business

2. trade reference   B. 商界 / 同行证明   b. a company that supplies information for other companies

3. financial standing   C. 资金   c. the ability to manage a company

4. enquiry agency   D. 财务状况   d. a statement given by a bank about the financial position of a business

5. confidential   E. 商务查询   e. money or property of a company

6. capital   F. 商务参赞处   f. a statement given by business partners about the financial position of a business

7. business enquiry	G. 业务能力	g. a group of local business people who work together to help business and trade in a particular town
8. chamber of commerce	H. 咨询社	h. private
9. commercial counselor's office	I. 银行证明	i. an official organization which represents its country abroad and advises companies on trade between the two countries
10. capacity	J. 私密的	j. an enquiry about business information

Part ② Case Study

In this part, you are supposed to read four letters on establishing business relations.

Letter 1: Buyer's request for establishing business relations

Situation: *Zhang Lin, a sales assistant from Guangdong Food Import and Export Company, was given a name card of Mr. Tstuna, the sales manager of Supreme Food Supply Co. Ltd. He attempts to get in touch with Mr. Tstuna in the hope of building up partnership and seeking for business opportunities.*

Dear Mr. Tstuna,

    Through the courtesy of the chamber of commerce in Tokyo, we have learned that you **specialize in** the best quality foods all over the world, and we are **in the market for** various exotic foods. We are writing to you in the hope of establishing business relations with you.

We are the largest food trading company in Guangdong, China, with offices or **representatives** in all major cities and towns in the country. We have been importing a large variety of foods from Europe and the USA and had **considerable** experience in this line.

A bright prospect for your products in our market is foreseeable, and we look forward to hearing from you and always **assure** you **of** our close cooperation.

Yours faithfully,

Zhang Lin

Letter 2: Seller's request for establishing business relations

Situation: *Luo Bin, a sales assistant in Guangdong Fashion Toys Import and Export Co. Ltd., exchanged his name card with that of Jesson, the sales manager of Kidsfun Toys Co. Ltd. from Tokyo, Japan at the Canton Fair. Afterwards, Mr. Luo writes an email to Jesson in the hope of entering into partnership and seeking for business opportunities.*

Dear Jesson,

I would like to express my sincere gratitude to you for taking time to visit our booth SH-68 at the Canton Fair this spring.

This is Bin from Guangdong Fashion Toys Import and Export Co. Ltd., which specializes in manufacturing various toys which are all excellent in quality. For more information, you can visit our website.

Enclosed are some of your photos at our booth, which I believe will remind you of our company and products. We would appreciate it if you could provide us with details of your requirements.

We would like to enter into business relations with you and now forward you the **quotation** sheet with some hot items **for your information**. You are also warmly welcomed to visit our company and communicate with us.

Looking forward to hearing from you.

Best regards,

Luo Bin

Letter 3: Seller's request for establishing business relations

Situation: *Wen Min, a sales manager in Guangdong Machinery Import and Export Co. Ltd., received a letter transferred from her colleague in Shanghai. She is glad to contact Mr. Johnson, the CEO of Golden Star Electric Co. Ltd. from Thailand. Ms. Wen writes an email to Johnson in the hope of seeking for business prospects.*

Dear Mr. Johnson,

Your letter of May 8th **addressed to** our sister corporation in Shanghai has been transferred to us for our attention. As the items fall within our **business scope**, we shall be pleased to enter into direct business relations with you.

We have learned that you are one of the **leading** importers and wholesalers of electric and electronic machinery and equipment in Thailand. We are exporters of the same **lines of business, boasting** a business background of some 40 years, and now particularly interested in exporting to your country electronic products of various types.

All kinds of our products are **good sellers** and worth recommendation for their excellent quality. If you are interested in **marketing** these products **at your end**, please let us know and we shall be pleased to send you our quotations and sample books upon receipt of your specific enquiry.

We look forward to your favorable reply.

Yours faithfully,

Wen Min

Letter 4: Buyer's request for establishing business relations

Situation: *Jeff Marshal, a sales manager of Elegance Garment Trading Company, was happy to get to know Zhongshan Guangming Textile Export Co. Ltd. through his bank in Lagos, Nigeria. He is searching for cotton products and willing to buy products regularly from suppliers with a good reputation.*

Dear Sirs,

We are writing to you in the hope of establishing business relations with you. We owe your name and address to Bank of China, Lagos Branch, through whom we have learned you are an exporter of Chinese textiles and cotton piece goods. For your information, textiles are our main imports, but now we are especially interested in importing printed shirting from your country.

If you can assure us of **workable prices**, **excellent quality** and **prompt delivery**, we shall be able to **deal in** these goods **on a substantial scale**. We would therefore highly appreciate it if you would send us by airmail catalogues, sample books and all necessary information regarding printed shirting, so as to acquaint us with the material and workmanship of your supplies.

We are looking forward to your early reply.

Yours faithfully,

Jeff Marshal

Words and Expressions

1. **through the courtesy of...** 承蒙……的（介绍，关照）

2. **specialize in** 专门从事，专营

3. **in the market for** 想要购买，拟购

4. **representative** *n.* 代表 *adj.* 典型的；有代表性的

5. **considerable** *adj.* 可观的；大量的

6. **assure...of...** 使……确信；向……保证

7. **enclosed** *adj.* 随函附上的

8. **quotation** *n.* 报价；估价

9. **for your information** 供你方参考

10. **addressed to** 写给（某人）的，说给（某人）的

11. **business scope** 经营范围

12. leading *adj.* 领先的，最前的

13. line of business 行业；业务范围

14. boast *v.* 有（值得自豪的东西）

15. good seller 热销品，畅销品；受欢迎的产品

16. market *v.* 推销，促销

17. at your end 在你方所在地

18. workable price 合理 / 可行的价格

19. excellent quality 质量上乘

20. prompt delivery 发货及时

21. deal in 经营

22. on a substantial scale 大规模地；大量地

Exercises

I. **Match the sentences with the key points of letters on establishing business relations and finish the table below.**

1. We owe your name and address to General Trading Company who has informed us that you are in the market for a wide range of foods.

2. We are a state-owned corporation, handling both the import and export of foods.

3. We avail ourselves of this opportunity to approach you for the establishment of trade relations with you.

4. We have been in the line of foods for more than 20 years.

5. We look forward to receiving your enquiries soon.

6. Through the courtesy of D&M, we learned that you specialize in the import of toys.

7. We look forward to a long and prosperous relationship with your company.

8. We sincerely hope to establish good business relations with your esteemed corporation.

Key Points of Letters on Establishing Business Relations	Sentences
Source of information	
Intention of writing the letter	
Introduction of the company	
Expectation	

 II. **Find the errors in the letter and improve it.**

May 12th, 2022

Dear Ito & Co., Ltd., Ginza, Tokyo.,

Anderson Company was build in 1998, we are a state-run enterprise responsible for the production and import and export of electronic toys. In this industry, we have 25 years experience. Our products are of very good quality and variety, and great repute.

If you are interested in our company, please let us know your trade terms, and we will send you forward samples. We really hope to establish good business relations with your corporation.

Looking forward to hear you soonest possible.

Yours sincerely,

Jeff

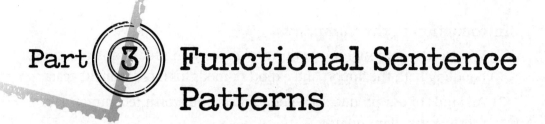

Part 3 Functional Sentence Patterns

1. Source of Information

(1) We come to know your name and address from the Commercial Counselor's Office of the Chinese Embassy in New York.

(2) Through the courtesy of the Chamber of Commerce in Tokyo, we have learned that you are in the market for foods.

(3) We owe your name and address to Walters Trading Company.

(4) Your firm has been introduced/recommended / passed on to us by D&G Company.

(5) We searched your company from Alibaba and knew that you deal in toys.

(6) Glad to have your name card at the Canton Fair.

2. Intention of Writing the Letter

(1) We are now writing to you for the establishment of business relations with you.

(2) We take the liberty of writing to you with a view to establishing business relations with you.

(3) As the items fall within our business scope, we shall be pleased to enter into direct business relations with you.

(4) The purpose of this letter is to explore the possibilities of developing trade relations with you.

(5) We are confident that a beneficial and friendly relationship can be established between our two companies.

(6) We'd like to express our desire to establish business relations with you on the basis of equality, mutual benefit, and the exchange of needed goods.

3. Introduction of the Company

(1) We are the largest food trading company in Guangdong, China, handling both the import and export of foods for more than 30 years.

(2) All kinds of our products are good sellers and worth recommendation for their excellent quality.

(3) We are a state-owned corporation of high reputation all over the world.

(4) We specialize in pianos and shall be glad to trade with you in this line.

(5) We are the largest distributor of household electrical appliances in China and we have enjoyed a wide popularity in the world market.

(6) We have many years' experience in foreign trade and the long-established direct factory connections allow us to become the most competitive firm in our line.

4. Expectation

(1) We look forward to receiving your enquiries soon.

(2) An early reply will be obliged.

(3) We await hearing from you soon.

(4) Your early reply will be much appreciated.

(5) We look forward to a long and prosperous relationship with your company.

(6) We hope to be favored with your cooperation.

Part 4 Situational Dialogs

Dialog 1: *At an exhibition, John Bobbie, the general manager of an importing company, comes to the booth of China Electronic Product Import and Export Company Ltd. where Zhou Feng is the sales manager. They exchange business cards and make a brief talk to establish business relations.*

John Bobbie: Good morning. My name is John Bobbie.

Zhou Feng: Good morning, Mr. Bobbie. My name is Zhou Feng, sales manager in my company. Here's my business card.

John Bobbie: Nice to meet you, Ms. Zhou. We've learned that you specialize in the export of electronic products.

Zhou Feng: Oh, yes. Will you please take a seat? Mr. Bobbie, have you seen the display of our electronic products in the exhibition hall downstairs?

John Bobbie: Yes. I had a look just now. I found some of the exhibits of excellent quality and beautiful design. I feel we might be able to do an important business together.

Zhou Feng: Sure, we can. You know, we've been in this line for more than 20 years. We are the largest distributor of electronic products in China and we have enjoyed a wide popularity in the world market.

John Bobbie: So, Ms. Zhou, we're a newly-established company, but we have wide connections with wholesalers and retailers all over America.

Zhou Feng: Good. Here is our catalog and pricelist.

John Bobbie: Thanks a lot. I'll read it carefully and pick out the items that we are interested in.

Zhou Feng: OK. We look forward to a long and prosperous relationship with your company.

Dialog 2: *After the exhibition, Zhou Feng made a follow-up call to John Bobbie.*

John Bobbie: Good morning. This is John Bobbie, Antarctic Modern Company in New York.

Zhou Feng: Good morning, Mr. Bobbie. This is Zhou Feng from China Electronic Product Import and Export Company Ltd. Thank you for visiting our booth in China.

John Bobbie: Oh, Zhou, I see. I took some photos in your booth; you are so nice.

Zhou Feng: Thanks. Are there any of our products interesting to you?

John Bobbie: Yes, I read your catalog carefully. And I find some of your goods are beautiful in design.

Zhou Feng: Sure. You will find all of our products are good sellers and worth recommendation for their excellent design and quality. Moreover, we have many years' experience in foreign trade and the long-established direct factory connections allow us to become the most competitive firm in our line.

John Bobbie: Thank you for your information. Would you please send us your samples? We can hold more talks on the details later when I have received your samples.

Zhou Feng: OK, samples will be sent to you soon. We are confident that a beneficial and friendly relationship can be established between our two companies.

Exercise

Work in pairs and make a business dialog with your partner on establishing business relations according to the information given in the cue cards.

Cue Card A

> You are Mr./Ms. Lin, an export salesperson from Canton Company in China. You need to:
> - send your greetings and indicate the source of information;
> - introduce your company;
> - show your thanks and promise to send catalogs and samples;
> - expect to enter into business relations.

Cue Card B

> You are Mr./Ms. Burne, an import manager from Random Company in the USA. You need to:
> - greet your partner;
> - show your interest in the products;
> - promise to give the best attention;
> - express goodwill.

Part ⑤ Skill Training

I. **Match the words and phrases in the left column with their translations in the right column.**

1. learn from   A. 报价

2. be in the market for   B. 大量的

3. electronic toy   C. 具体询盘

4. specialize in   D. 电子玩具

5. competitive price   E. 与……建立业务关系

6. make a quotation   F. 从……获知

7. considerable   G. 想要购买

8. specific enquiry   H. 专门经营……

9. business line   I. 业务范围

10. establish business relations with...   J. 具有竞争力的价格

II. **Fill in the blanks with appropriate words or phrases given in the box.**

catalog	specializing in	excellent quality	in the market for
learned from	enquiries	for more information	establish

Dear Sirs,

    We **1.** _____ the website that you are **2.** _____ _____ electronic toys.

    This is Guangzhou Liuhe Co., Ltd. **3.** _____ the manufacture and export of toys. Our products are all with **4.** _____.
5. _____, please visit our website to have a further understanding of us.

If you need our 6. _____, please send me your 7. _____ by email. We sincerely hope to 8. _____ business relations with your esteemed corporation.

Yours sincerely,

Bill

III. **Choose the best answer to complete each of the following sentences.**

1. We would _____ very much if you send us a few sample books.

A. appreciated   B. appreciate it

C. appreciate you   D. appreciate

2. We will send to you a copy of our export list _____ the main items available at present.

A. covered   B. covering

C. cover   D. are covered

3. We would like to receive your enquiries _____ our hardware.

A. about   B. to

C. for   D. into

4. We wish to establish direct business relations _____ you.

A. with   B. for

C. from   D. to

5. We are planning to _____ our business activities to our neighboring countries.

A. execute   B. extend

C. extension   D. enlarging

6. We are _____ your detailed requirements.

A. forwarding   B. looking to

C. looking forward   D. looking forward to

7. We are interested in your cotton piece goods and wish to receive your _____ soon.

    A. specific enquiry   B. special enquiry

    C. specific enquire   D. enquire specifically

8. We are writing to you _____ you can give us the lowest quotation.

    A. hope   B. hoping to

    C. in the hope that   D. in the hope of

9. We _____ make business contact with you.

    A. desirous to   B. desire

    C. are desirous to   D. are desirous of

10. On the _____ of Changsha Trading Company, we know your name and address.

    A. requirement   B. recommendation

    C. recommend   D. demands

IV. **Translate the following sentences into English or Chinese respectively.**

1. 我公司是拉各斯市（Lagos）最大的电器用品进口商，主要经营电器用品进口业务。

2. 我们从史密斯先生处得知你方的名称与地址，他与我们做了很多年的生意。

3. 我们想利用这个机会介绍一下我们的业务范围。

4. 作为对我公司的介绍，随函附上我方秋季宣传册供你方参考。

5. 我方寄给你方现可供应的各种自行车的价格表。

6. We are in the market for your cotton piece goods.

7. We are a state-owned corporation of high reputation all over the world.

8. We have an interest in your waterproof garments and would like to obtain your quotation and information concerning the designs, colors, materials, etc.

9. We are indebted your address to Nagoya Industry, who informed us that you are in the market for chemicals.

10. If you're interested in any type of these items, please don't hesitate to tell us.

Ⅴ. Write a business letter according to the following situation.

You are an importer of electronic goods in Japan. Recently you got a piece of information about Top Electronic Products Co., Ltd. in China on the Internet. Write a letter to ask for establishing business relations.

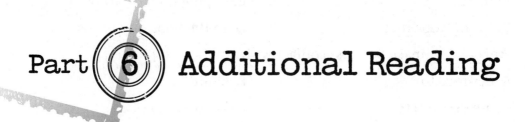

Part 6 Additional Reading

What Are Yellow Pages?

The term *yellow pages* is used to refer to the business section of a telephone directory, which is conventionally separated from the residential section in large cities. The separation of business and residential listings in a telephone directory appears to have originated in the United States, which began using and referring to the yellow pages in the early part of the 20th century. Since then, the concept has spread to other nations, including those that do not speak English, and in some countries, it is a branded term, rather than a generic one.

The idea of an alphabetized telephone directory which covered a certain geographical region also originated in Connecticut, US, in 1878. Along with names and phone numbers, the directory typically included the address of the telephone subscriber, along with his or her profession. Less than 20 years later, most telephone directories were separated into business and residential listings, allowing consumers to look up businesses by name or type, and the separation began to be indicated with pages printed on yellow paper, rather than white paper typically used for residential listings.

Originally, yellow pages took the form that white pages did, with a series of alphabetically arranged listings in an easy to read, uniformly sized typeface. However, directory publishers quickly realized the advertising potential, and most modern yellow pages offer advertising opportunities. Businesses can increase or bold the typeface used for their company, as well as presenting ads within the yellow pages section to attract consumers' attention.

Many telephone directories also allow ads or text in color to further draw the eye.

Generally, the yellow pages of a phone book are distributed free to all telephone subscribers within the area. To look something up in the yellow pages, the consumer typically searches by business types. For example, if someone needs new glasses, he or she would look up "optometrists" in the yellow pages. In some cases, the yellow pages also include an alphabetical listing of all of the businesses in the area, so that a consumer can look up a specific business.

The term has also jumped to the Internet, in the form of online yellow pages, namely business directory websites which allow people to find listed businesses all over the nation. A number of websites provide online yellow pages, usually networking with several phone companies and allowing businesses to place advertisements and provide more information about themselves, including a web address.

Chapter 3

Enquiry

Learning Objectives

By completing this unit, students will learn:

- what an enquiry is in international business and how to make an enquiry;
- how to analyze case letters on enquiries and replies;
- useful expressions and sentence patterns related to enquiries;
- how to negotiate on enquiries.

Lead-in

Work in groups, discuss the following questions and then share your answers with the whole class.

1. What is an enquiry in international business?

2. What are the differences between specific enquiries and general enquiries?

3. What are the main parts of letters on making enquiries?

4. What should you pay attention to when writing letters on making enquiries?

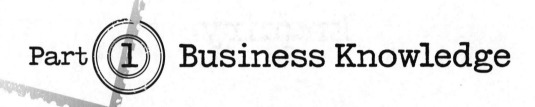

Part ① Business Knowledge

Section 1 What Is an Enquiry in International Business?

Making an enquiry is the first real step in business negotiation after establishing business relations between two companies. In international business the importer may send an enquiry to an exporter, inviting a quotation and/or an offer for the goods he wishes to buy or simply asking for some general information about these goods. However, it is made without engagement.

An enquiry can be divided into two categories: general enquiry and specific enquiry. A general enquiry refers to the importer's request for some general information about the goods produced by the exporter; it is not very concrete. In most cases, the importer only asks for samples, catalogs, brochures, or pricelists while sometimes he may also intend to know something on the quality, quantity, price, and delivery date.

A specific enquiry refers to the importer's request for specific information. However, if the importer is a regular customer, he would only request for the name, quality, quantity, and price of the goods since he has already known the other terms and conditions needed for the transaction. On the other hand, if the importer is new to the exporter, he would ask for all the trade terms, like the name of the goods, quality, quantity, discounts, insurance, payment terms, shipment, and so on.

Exercises

I. **Read the passage and choose the best answer to each question.**

1. An enquiry is usually made by the _____.

   A. manufacturer   B. end-user

   C. exporter   D. importer

2. When making an enquiry, the importer would be interested in the following facts about products EXCEPT _____.

   A. price   B. specification

   C. shipment   D. development

3. According to the passage, how many kinds of enquiries are mentioned?

   A. One.   B. Two.

   C. Three.   D. Four.

4. In a specific enquiry, _____.

   A. the importer asks for samples, catalogs, or pricelists

   B. the importer intends to know the basic knowledge of the products in general

   C. the importer would ask for specific information on all the trade terms if he has never done business with the exporter before

   D. the importer has already decided to buy a product

5. Which of the following statements is true according to the passage?

   A. An enquiry letter is usually made by the seller to the buyer.

   B. The specific enquiry should always be made in a detailed way.

   C. Sometimes the enquiry would bind on both the exporter and the importer.

   D. The enquiry is made without engagement.

II. Decide whether the statements are true (T) or false (F) according to the passage.

1. Making an enquiry is a necessary step before establishing business relations between two companies. (   )

2. An enquiry can be divided into two kinds: general enquiry and personal enquiry. (   )

3. In a general enquiry, the importer only requests for some general information about the goods produced by the exporter. (   )

4. It is generally not a regular customer but a new customer that makes an enquiry. (   )

Section 2 How to Make an Enquiry

An enquiry is made to seek a supply of products, services, or information. In order to obtain the needed information, the enquirer should state simply, clearly, and concisely what he wants—general information, like a catalog or pricelist, a sample, a quotation, etc. Therefore, enquiries should be specific and provide the necessary details to enable the receiver to answer the questions completely.

If both parties have never dealt with each other before, the importer should inform the exporter of the source of information at the beginning of the letter, i.e., how he learned about the company or the products. Details of his own company and/or business scope will also be included. Such kind of letter is known as a "First Enquiry". On the other hand, if the importer is the exporter's regular customer, the importer would ask for information directly, such as the goods and services he is interested in, or any terms and conditions needed for a transaction.

The reply to an enquiry should be prompt and courteous and cover all the information asked for. If it is from an regular customer, say how much you appreciate it; if it is from a new customer, say you are glad to receive it and express the hope of keeping a friendly business relationship.

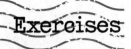

Exercises

I. **Read the passage and answer the following questions.**

1. What is the purpose of making enquiries?

_____

2. What is the principle of making enquiries?

_____

3. What is a "first enquiry"?

_____

4. Under what circumstances can the importer ask for information directly?

_____

5. What is the principle of making a reply to an enquiry?

_____

II. **Decide whether the statements are true (T) or false (F) according to the passage.**

1. It is not essential for the enquirer to state what he wants clearly and concisely. (   )

2. The importer always informs the exporter of the source of information at the beginning of an enquiry letter. (   )

3. The importer should introduce his own company and/or business scope in the first enquiry. (   )

4. In reply to an enquiry, you can say you are glad to receive it and express the hope of keeping a friendly business relationship. (   )

Part  Case Study

In this part, you are supposed to read four letters on enquiries and replies.

Letter 1: A general enquiry

Situation: *Luo Ying is a sales manager in Guangzhou Textile Company. Her friend recommended British Fashion Company to her, so she is writing an enquiry letter to the sales manager of the company for a copy of catalog.*

Dear Mr. George,

Through the courtesy of Messrs. Menn & Smith of Washington, we learned that you are an exporter of all cotton bed sheets. We are **making an enquiry** for your cotton products. We would like you to send us your **illustrated catalogs**, pricelists, and samples, giving us a general idea of your products.

We are one of the leading dealers in textiles and there is **a steady demand** here **for a wide range of** cotton products. We believe **substantial business** could be **materialized** if your price is **moderate**.

Your early reply is appreciated.

Yours faithfully,

Luo Ying

Letter 2: A specific enquiry

Situation: *Hyman, a sales manager of Elegance Garment Trading Company, learned about Shenzhen Textile Export Co. Ltd. at the Canton Fair. He is asking Xiao Min, the sales director of the latter company, for quotation, samples, and so on.*

Dear Xiao Min,

We are one of the leading importers of sweaters in New York. We have seen your products displayed at the Canton Fair.

At present, we are interested in your men's sweaters very much, especially in the Art. No. SC-123. Will you please **quote** us the lowest price based on CIF New York, **inclusive of** our 6% **commission**, stating the earliest date of shipment and terms of payment?

We would appreciate it if you could provide us with samples of different colors upon receipt of the letter.

Should your price be competitive and delivery date acceptable, we will **place an order with** you.

Your early reply will be appreciated.

Yours faithfully,

Hyman

Letter 3: Reply to an enquiry

Situation: *George, the sales manager of British Fashion Company, received Luo Ying's enquiry from Guangzhou Textile Company. Now George is writing a reply to Luo Ying in the hope of receiving the first order.*

Dear Luo Ying,

We are very pleased to receive your enquiry of May 20th and have enclosed our illustrated catalog and pricelist, giving you a general idea of our products. Also, by **separate post**, we are sending you some samples and feel confident that when you have examined them, you will agree the goods are both **excellent in quality and reasonable in price**.

Our **regular purchases** are in quantities of not less than 100 dozen for each item. To show our sincerity, we would allow you a discount of 2% for this **initial order**. Payment is to be made by **irrevocable** L/C at sight.

Because of their softness and durability, our cotton bed sheets are rapidly becoming popular and the demand for our products keeps rising year by year. But if you place your order not later than the end of this month, we would ensure prompt shipment.

We invite your attention to our other products such as table cloths and table napkins, and look forward to receiving your first order.

Best regards,

George

Letter 4: Reply to an enquiry

Situation: *Wu Qing, a sales manager in Shenzhen Textile Export Co. Ltd., received a letter from Hyman, a sales manager of Elegance Garment Trading Company. Ms. Wu writes a reply to Hyman in response to his enquiry letter for product information.*

Dear Hyman,

We are honored to note from your letter dated May 21st that, as one of the major importers of garment products, you are interested in our men's sweaters.

As requested, we have pleasure in sending you a copy of the catalog and samples of different colors and prices based on CIF New York. We give 5% discount on orders of more than $15,000. Our usual payment is made by irrevocable letter of credit at sight and the shipment can be effected in August.

We hope the catalog gives you all the information you need, but please do not hesitate to tell us if you would like any further details.

We trust you would give us an early reply.

Yours faithfully,

Wu Qing

Words and Expressions

1. **make an enquiry** 询盘

2. **illustrated catalog** 带有插图的目录

3. **a steady demand for...** 对……有稳定的需求

4. **a wide range of** 一系列的，各种各样的

5. **substantial business** 大生意

6. **materialize** *v.* 成交；实现

7. **moderate** *adj.* 适度的，中等的；合理的

8. quote *v.* 报价

9. inclusive of 包含的，包括……在内的

10. commission *n.* 佣金

11. place an order with... 向……下订单

12. separate post 另外邮寄

13. excellent in quality and reasonable in price 物美价廉

14. regular purchase 定期采购

15. initial order 首批订单

16. irrevocable L/C 不可撤销信用证

17. as requested 应要求

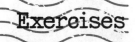

Exercises

I. **Match the sentences with the key points of letters on enquiries and finish the table below.**

1. We have seen your products displayed at the Canton Fair.

2. It would be helpful if you could send us samples, and if they are of the standard we require, we will place a substantial order.

3. Messrs. Menn & Green informs us that you are an exporter of cotton bed sheets.

4. We would like you to send us your illustrated catalogs, pricelists, and samples, giving us a general idea of your products.

5. We are one of the leading importers of sweaters in New York.

6. We would appreciate it if you could provide us with samples of different colors upon receipt of the letter.

7. We are the largest food trading company in Guangdong, China, handling both the import and export of foods for more than 30 years.

Key Points of Letters on Enquiries	Sentences
Source of information	
Introduction of the company	
Intention of writing the letter	

II. Find the errors in the letter and improve it.

May 24th, 2022

Dear Sir,

Hi, this is the biggest company in America. We have customers in the world. But we want to expand our business in European.

We hope to have as many partners as possible. If you want to be our partner, you have to give us a better quotation, commission, some samples, and catalogs.

In a word, our company want to do business with you. We are awaiting for your answer.

Yours sincerely,

Jerry

Part ③ Functional Sentence Patterns

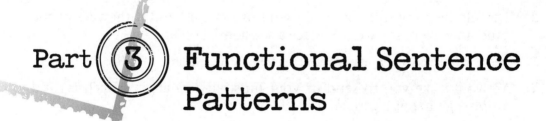

1. **Introduction of the Company**

   (1) We are a leading company with many years' experience in the import of cotton articles.

   (2) We enjoy a good reputation internationally in the circle of electronic goods.

   (3) We would like to introduce us as one of the leading importers of cotton articles in America.

   (4) Owing to the superior quality, attractive design, and reasonable price, our products sell well all over the world.

(5) We have been in the line of cotton goods for many years.

(6) We are introducing this with pride and pleasure and can bring you very stylish and cost-effective cotton goods.

2. Intention of Writing the Letter

(1) Please send us three copies of your latest catalog at your earliest convenience.

(2) We would appreciate your sending us a catalog of your men's sweaters together with terms of payment and the largest discount you can allow us.

(3) Full information as to prices, quality, quantity available, and other relevant details are appreciated.

(4) Upon receipt of this letter, please send us some samples of your products and two copies of brochure as soon as possible.

(5) We prefer CIF price, so please quote us a price on that basis.

(6) Please let us know your price for the goods advertised in yesterday's *New York Times* and the earliest possible date of delivery.

3. Reply to an Enquiry

(1) Enclosed please find a pricelist for our new product line.

(2) The prices quoted include your 3% commission for orders exceeding USD1,800.

(3) Please find enclosed a full range of catalogs covering the steel tableware enquired in your letter of May 4th.

(4) We have much pleasure in enclosing a quotation sheet for our products and trust that their high quality will induce you to place a trial order.

(5) We wish to extend the sales of our products to your market and are sending you our quotation with the hope that you will recommend them to the prospective clients.

(6) We would like very much to do business with you and now await your first order.

Part ④ Situational Dialogs

Dialog 1: *Li Hai, the general manager of purchase department of a company in Guangdong, is making an enquiry to Eric Mathew, the manager of a machine tools factory in the UK. They have previously made a phone call to meet each other.*

Li Hai: Excuse me, are you Eric? I'm Li Hai. We talked on the phone earlier.

Eric Mathew: Yes. Nice to meet you. Please come in. Would you like something to drink?

Li Hai: Nice to meet you, too. Water is OK. Thank you.

Eric Mathew: You are welcome. I was informed that you are interested in our machine tools. Is that right?

Li Hai: Yes. We saw your advertisement on the Internet, and are thinking of placing an order. But will you give me an introduction of your factory?

Eric Mathew: Of course. Our factory is one of the largest machine tools factories in the UK. It has its own workplace, advanced technology, and intellectual property.

Li Hai: I see. How about your products? We would appreciate your giving us an illustrated catalog.

Eric Mathew: Our products are easy to operate and durable in use. Here is our illustrated catalog.

Li Hai: Oh, wonderful. Then, have you got a product of this specification?

Eric Mathew: Let me see. Yes, we have. We supply machine tools of all designs and sizes.

Li Hai: That's so good. Can you assure us of your regular supply?

Eric Mathew: No problem. I hope we can cooperate happily.

Li Hai: I'm sure we will.

Eric Mathew: Waiting for your first order.

Dialog 2: *Ms. Shy, the import manager of Ocean Company Ltd., wants to make an enquiry for women's dresses. Now Keven, sales representative of Guangzhou Youmi Textile Trade Co. Ltd., is talking about it with her.*

Shy: Hello, I searched your company from Alibaba. We are aware of your fine reputation in manufacturing dresses. We are very interested in your women's dresses. What kind of material are they made of?

Keven: Thank you for your enquiry. Our women's dresses are made of super pure silk and with traditional skills.

Shy: Do you have different colors for the same style?

Keven: Besides red and white, we also customize yellow and green, but the price will be a little higher. What do you think of our products?

Shy: I think they are fashionable and suit European ladies well, too. It would also be helpful if you could send us samples.

Keven: Sure, samples would be forwarded to you tomorrow. And we have much pleasure in enclosing a quotation sheet for our products and trust that their high quality and competitive price will induce you to place a trial order.

Shy: Thanks. If they are of high quality and reasonable prices, we'll purchase large quantities of them.

Keven: Your early reply will be much appreciated.

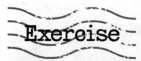

Exercise

Work in pairs and make a business dialog with your partner on making and replying to an enquiry according to the information given in the cue cards.

Cue Card A

You are Mr./Ms. Yang, from a computer import company. You need to:
- Know the quality of the computers;
- ask for information on Model 3012;
- ask for price and available quantity;
- express appreciation and promise to call for further information.

Cue Card B

> You are Mr./Ms. Ben, from a computer export company. You need to:
> - show your appreciation and confirm the quality of your goods;
> - promise to send the catalog on Model 3012;
> - give information on price and current supply from stock;
> - expect to do business together.

Part ⑤ Skill Training

I. **Match the words and phrases in the left column with their translations in the right column.**

1. place an order with...   A. 定期采购

2. irrevocable L/C   B. 大订单

3. regular purchase   C. 一系列的……

4. a wide range of...   D. 不可撤销信用证

5. commission   E. 向……下订单

6. catalog   F. 交货时间

7. in the line of...   G. 佣金

8. delivery date   H. 样品

9. sample   I. 在……行业

10. substantial business   J. 产品目录

II. **Fill in the blanks with appropriate words or phrases given in the box.**

orders	high quality	conclude
enquiring	sending	payment

Dear Sirs,

Thank you for your letter of June 24th, **1.** _____ about our "Gesundheit" cloth.

We have much pleasure in **2.** _____ you a copy of the catalog and samples of the full range of colors and the prices and trust that their **3.** _____ will induce you to place a trial order. We give 3% discount on **4.** _____ of $50,000 or more, and **5.** _____ must be made by irrevocable letter of credit at sight. We should be very pleased to **6.** _____ business with you.

We hope the catalog gives all the information you need, but please do not hesitate to write again if you would like any further details.

Yours sincerely,

Daisy He

III. Choose the best answer to complete each of the following sentences.

1. Please let us have the details of your "Panda" brand color TV sets, _____ us your earliest delivery.

    A. give   B. to give

    C. giving   D. given

2. We are sure that we will place _____ orders with you.

    A. consider   B. considerable

    C. considerate   D. considering

3. We'd like to take this _____ to introduce ourselves as one of the leading importers in our country.

    A. possibility   B. time

    C. occasion   D. opportunity

4. We await _____ from you.

    A. hear   B. hearing

    C. to hear   D. to hearing

5. We hope to receive your quotation with details _____ the earliest date of shipment.

    A. including   B. to be included

    C. being included   D. include

6. Should your prices _____ found competitive, we intend to place an order with you.

    A. is   B. be

    C. are   D. to be

7. We shall appreciate _____ us CIF Melbourne.

    A. you quote   B. you to quote

    C. your quoting   D. to you quoting

8. Quotations and samples will be sent _____ receipt of your specific enquiry.

    A. for   B. upon

    C. with   D. to

9. As this article falls _____ the scope of our business activities, we take this opportunity to express our wish to conduct some transactions with you in the near future.

    A. with   B. in

    C. within   D. at

10. Please send us your _____ catalog, together with samples and pricelist.

    A. illustrate   B. illustrated

    C. illustrating   D. illustration

IV. **Translate the following sentences into English or Chinese respectively.**

1. 如果贵方寄来商品目录、报价单及其他相关信息，我们将非常感谢。

2. 对于超过 10 000 件的订单我方将给予 10% 的折扣。

3. 从你方 8 月 30 日的信中获悉，你方对我方的新产品感兴趣。

4. 应你方要求，兹报 123 号商品 FOB 上海的最低价以供参考。

5. 我们要求的货物应经久耐用、色彩鲜艳。

6. Please let us know the price for the toys as advertised in yesterday's *New York Times*, and the earliest possible date of delivery.

7. Please send us three copies of your latest catalog at your earliest convenience.

8. Would you please give me a general idea of your business scope?

9. We may place regular orders for large quantities if your quality is suitable and the prices are competitive.

10. We are very much interested in your products, and would appreciate it if you could let us have information as to prices, quantity available, and other relative details.

V. Write a business letter according to the following situation.

Write to ABC Company to make a specific enquiry for the following products and request the exporter to quote prices on the basis of CIF Montreal.

1. 100% cotton cloth, color NO. 12, standard width, 200 yards.

2. Silk of 20% nylon, color NO. 5, standard width, 200 yards.

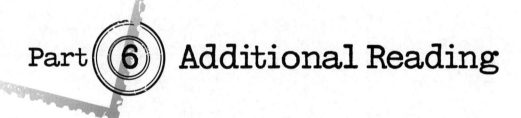

Part 6 Additional Reading

Business-to-Business (B2B)

Business-to-business (B2B), also called B-to-B, refers to business that is conducted between companies, rather than between a company and individual consumers. Business-to-business stands in contrast to business-to-consumer (B2C) and business-to-government (B2G) transactions. The following are the features of B2B.

- B2B is a transaction or business conducted between one business and another, such as a wholesaler and a retailer.

- B2B transactions tend to happen in the supply chain, where one company will purchase raw materials from another to be used in the manufacturing process.

- B2B transactions are also commonplace for auto industry companies, as well as property management, housekeeping, and industrial cleanup companies.

The Internet provides a robust environment in which businesses can find out about products and services and lay the groundwork for future business-to-business transactions.

Company websites allow interested parties to learn about a business' products and services and initiate contact. Online product and supply exchange websites allow businesses to search for products and services and initiate procurement through e-procurement interfaces. Specialized online directories providing information about particular industries, companies, and the products and services they provide also facilitate B2B transactions.

In 2020, the global B2B ecommerce market was valued at $14.9 trillion—over five times that of the B2C market. On top of that, Forrester predicts that B2B ecommerce will account for 17% of all B2B sales in the US by 2023, reaching $1.8 trillion. Needless to say, B2B ecommerce is reaching new heights.

Chapter 4

Offer and Counter Offer

Learning Objectives

By completing this unit, students will learn:

- types of offers and features of counter offers;
- how to analyze case letters on offers and counter offers;
- useful expressions and functional sentence patterns related to offers and counter offers;
- how to negotiate on offers and counter offers.

Lead-in

Work in groups, discuss the following questions and then share your answers with the whole class.

1. On what occasions does the offeror make a firm offer and when does he or she make a non-firm offer?

2. What key points are usually included when you write an offer letter?

3. Who usually makes the offer and who usually makes the counter offer?

4. What key points are usually included when you write a counter offer letter?

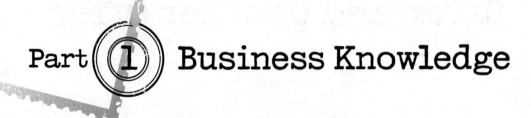

Part ① Business Knowledge

Section 1   Offer, Firm Offer and Non-firm Offer

An offer is a promise to supply goods on the terms and conditions stated. In an offer, the seller not only quotes the price of the goods he wishes to sell but also indicates all necessary terms of sales for the buyer's consideration and acceptance.

According to the United Nations Convention on Contracts for the International Sale of Goods (联合国国际货物销售合同), the definition of an offer is as follows: A proposal for concluding a contract addressed to one or more specific persons constitutes an offer if it is sufficiently definite and indicates the intention of the offeror to be bound in case of acceptance. The one who makes the offer is called offeror, and the one who receives the offer is called offeree.

An offer consists of two categories: firm offer and non-firm offer. A firm offer clearly expresses the offeror's willingness in concluding a contract. Such an offer will be binding on the offeror if the offer is accepted by the offeree. It has the following features: It includes all the necessary items for a transaction; it specifies the time by which the offer is valid and the time when the acceptance must be received; it uses the phrase "offer firm" indicating that the offer is made without reservations. For example, in a firm offer we usually get such phrases like "...subject to your reply reaching us by/before/within..." and "This offer is firm (open, valid, good) for...days".

A non-firm offer has not expressed the offeror's clear willingness to conclude a contract, thus making it possible for the offeror to get favorable conditions by adapting himself to the changing market and choosing the best chance of reaching an agreement. It has the following features: It does not necessarily include all the details needed for a transaction; it has reservations to the offer as indicated in phrases like "subject to our final confirmation" and "for reference only"; it does not have a time limit for acceptance since it is indicative only.

Exercises

I. **Read the passage and decide whether each of the following sentences belongs to a firm offer or a non-firm offer.**

1. We are making you, subject to your acceptance before the end of this month, the under-mentioned offer. (   )

2. Our offer is subject to change without notice. (   )

3. Our offer is subject to goods being unsold. (   )

4. Our offer is subject to your confirmation reaching here on or before the 25th this month. (   )

5. We offer you, subject to our final confirmation, the following goods. (   )

6. Our offer is subject to prior sale. (   )

7. Our offer is subject to your reply reaching here by August 14th, Beijing time. (   )

8. Our offer is valid for 30 days from today. (   )

II. Read the following two letters, decide whether each of them belongs to a firm offer or a non-firm offer, and then underline the typical sentence that makes each letter a firm offer or a non-firm offer.

Letter 1

Dear Sirs,

Thank you for your enquiry of May 15th for men's sweaters.

In reply, we make a firm offer for 1,500 pieces of men's sweaters at USD 25 per piece CIF New York, subject to your reply reaching us by May 20th. Shipment is to be made within two months upon receipt of your order. Payment is by L/C at sight.

As you are aware that there has been lately a brisk demand for the above commodities, such growing demand has doubtlessly resulted in increased prices. However, you may avail yourself of the opportunity to strengthen the market. Please note that we have quoted our most favorable price and aren't able to entertain any counter offer.

We are anticipating your reply.

Yours truly,

Samantha

Letter 2

Dear Sir,

With reference to your enquiry of May 16th, we take pleasure in making the following offer: 1,800 sets of color TV, at USD 160.00 per set CIF Montreal for shipment effected within 40 days after receipt of L/C for payment, which we hope you will find in order. Please note that this offer is subject to goods being unsold.

As we have received a large number of orders from other importers, we advise you to take immediate acceptance.

Yours truly,

Sara Warrant

Section 2 Counter Offer

A counter offer occurs when an offeree thinks that the offer is mostly acceptable, if certain terms or conditions are amended or changed according to his or her proposal. For example, he or she may find the price offered is higher than expected, and he or she may also think that terms like the shipment, payment, and packing should be changed. In this case, a counter offer occurs.

A counter offer is a reply to an offer which purports to be acceptance but contains additions, limitations, or other modifications. It is virtually a partial rejection of the original offer and also a counter proposal initiated by the offeree. He or she may show disagreement to the price, packing, or shipment, or would suggest some changes of the terms and conditions in the offer made by the offeror and state his or her own terms instead.

Exercises

I. Decide whether the statements are true (T) or false (F) according to the passage.

1. An offeror may think that the offer is mostly acceptable. (   )

2. A counter offer occurs whenever an offeree disagrees to certain terms. (   )

3. A counter offer purports to be acceptance. (   )

4. A counter offer is virtually a partial rejection of the original offer and also a counter suggestion initiated by the buyer. (   )

5. The buyer may show disagreement to a variety of aspects, such as the price, packing, shipment, etc. (   )

II. Identify the aspect of disagreement listed in each sentence.

1. Thank you for your letter of June 10th. We regret to say that we cannot accept your offer, as your time of delivery is too distant. (   )

2. It is true we have dealt with you on sight draft basis so far, and our business dealings have been satisfactory to both of us. We feel that we are entitled to easier terms. For this deal, we'd like to propose that you

draw on us 30 days after sight, documents against acceptance, instead of sight draft. (   )

3. We appreciate the good quality of these handbags, but unfortunately your prices appear to be on the high side. (   )

4. We do not see any advantage in your quotations, and would like to know whether you have any better value to offer. (   )

5. This is our trial order; we need to test our market response. It would be appreciated if you could lower minimum order quantity for us from 5,000 pcs to 3,000. (   )

Part ② Case Study

In this part, you are supposed to read letters on making offers and counter offers.

Letter 1: Offer

Situation: *Wen, a sales manager of Guangdong Electric Import and Export Co. Ltd., received an email from Johnson, the general manager of Golden Star Electric Co. Ltd. from Britain, asking for an offer for washing machines. In reply, Wen makes the following offer.*

Dear Johnson,

In response to your email of May 30th, we have sent you a reply by email this morning. You might have noted from our email that we **are** now **in a position to make** you a firm **offer** for 850 sets of washing machines at $580.00 per set CIF London, for shipment to be effected within two months after receipt of your order, and payment is to be made by sight L/C. This offer **is subject to** your reply reaching here within one week.

As you may be aware, there has been **an active demand for** washing machines in the market. Therefore, it is impossible for us to **keep this offer**

open too long, for it will result in an increased price, to which we hope you will pay attention, and meanwhile we are expecting your early reply.

Yours faithfully,

Wen

Letter 2: Counter offer

Situation: *Johnson, the general manager of Golden Star Electric Co. Ltd. from Britain, is writing a counter-offer letter to Wen, a sales manager of Guangdong Electric Import and Export Co. Ltd., in hopes of reducing the price to the level he is pleased with.*

Dear Wen,

We highly appreciate your offer of June 4th for 850 sets of washing machines.

However, we regret our inability to accept your offer, since our clients consider your price rather **on the high side**, and **out of line with** the **prevailing market level**. As you know, there are various famous quality brands such as Little Swan, Haier, Meiling and so on, which have already gained broad recognition in our market. After careful comparison, it's estimated that similar products from these big brands are almost priced at a lower level than your washing machines. We admit that your products are **novel in design and durable in use**, but they still need a competitive price to win our end users here.

In view of this, our clients ask for a 6% discount off your quotation. As there is keen competition in the market, I advise you to accept our counter offer.

We look forward to your favorable reply.

Yours faithfully,

Johnson

Letter 3: Offer

Situation: *Min is a sales assistant from China National Import and Export Corporation. He has received an enquiry for raincoats from Tycon Outdoor Products Trading Company and is writing a letter to make an offer for light-weight raincoats.*

Dear Sir,

We have received your enquiry for light-weight raincoats dated May 30th with many thanks. We are very pleased to tell you that our new model A205 is quite popular with clients from America and some European countries. It is made of supreme water-proof, yet breathable material and gives the human body extra comfort even in heavy rain. We have been receiving **repeat orders**, so we can assure you of high quality for this product. As requested, we take pleasure in making the following offer based on 10,000 pieces.

Item: Men's Hoodie Raincoat A205

Unit price: USD 5.00 per piece FOB Guangzhou

Packing: 6 dozen to a carton **lined with** plastic sheet

Lead time: 10 days

Payment: L/C at sight

Shipment: to be effected within 20 days after receipt of the L/C

Please note that this price is subject to goods being unsold, as they are soon **running out of stock** and the price of raw material is **on the rise** recently. We suggest that you take advantage of this **favorable offer** or the price might **soar up** soon.

Awaiting your early acceptance.

Yours sincerely,

Min

Letter 4: Counter offer

Situation: *Jerry, the sales manager of Tycon Outdoor Products Trading Company, is writing a counter-offer letter to Min, a sales assistant from China National Import and Export Corporation, in hopes of reducing the minimum quantity and shortening the lead time.*

Dear Min,

Thank you for your offer of June 5th and the samples under separate covers.

We appreciate your promptness in sending the samples and I am very happy to find them up to our customers' satisfaction. While agreeing on other terms of your offer, we'd like to draw your attention to the **minimum order quantity** and lead time you proposed.

Ten thousand for minimum quantity is a much bigger number than our any other orders, considering our small market here in Indonesia, so we'd suggest you cut the number to 5,000 pieces. In addition, we hope that you could speed up production and shorten the lead time. We hope to receive them the earliest possible and would appreciate your guarantee of delivery within two weeks after receipt of our L/C. We then need time to distribute and display the goods to each chain store. We'd be extremely grateful to you for a smaller minimum quantity and shorter lead time.

We look forward to your immediate reply.

Yours faithfully,

Jerry

Words and Expressions

1. **be in a position to do sth.** 有能力做某事

2. **make an offer** 报盘，发盘

3. **be subject to...** 以……为准，以……为有效

4. **an active demand for sth.** 对某物的活跃（旺盛）需求

5. **keep this offer open** 使该盘有效

6. **on the high side** 价格偏高

7. **out of line with** 与……不相符合

8. **prevailing market level** 现有的市场水平

9. **novel in design and durable in use** 设计新颖且经久耐用

10. **repeat order** 重复订单

11. **lined with...** 用……做内衬

12. **lead time** 生产周期

13. **run out of stock** 库存清空 / 售罄

14. **on the rise** 处于上升（阶段）

15. **favorable offer** 优惠的报盘

16. **soar up** 飞速上涨

17. **minimum order quantity (MOQ)** 最低订购量

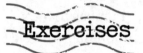

Exercises

I. Match the sentences with the key points of letters on making an offer and finish the table below.

1. We have received your enquiry for light-weight raincoats dated May 30th with thanks.

2. As we have been receiving a rush of orders now, we would advise you to place your order as soon as possible.

3. This offer is firm, subject to your reply reaching here before December 31st.

4. Replying to your enquiry of May 8th, we have the pleasure of quoting our brocade handbags as follows.

5. As for the above offer, it is extremely probable that the prices will still rise more, and it would therefore be to your interest to place your order without delay.

6. These quotations are all subject to the fluctuation of the market, and we hope to have your definite order, for we cannot keep our goods being unsold.

7. We are making you a firm offer for 850 sets of washing machines at $580.00 per set CIF London, and payment is to be made by sight L/C.

8. Our new model A205 is quite popular with clients from America and some European countries. It is made of supreme water-proof, yet breathable material and gives the human body extra comfort even in heavy rain.

Key Points of Letters on Making an Offer	Sentences
Confirm receipt of the enquiry	
Make an offer (indicate the terms and conditions)	
Indicate the validity of the offer	
Advertise the quality of the goods	
Persuade/expect the offeree to accept the offer	

II. **Match the sentences with the key points of letters on making a counter offer and finish the table below.**

1. Your competitors are offering considerably lower prices, and unless you can reduce your quotations, we shall have to buy elsewhere.

2. We regret that the price is not acceptable though we've both been making great efforts in concluding this transaction so far.

3. May I suggest that you could perhaps make some allowance on your quoted prices that would help to introduce your goods to our customers?

4. Thank you for your reply to our enquiry, quoting us the Chinese brocade handbags.

5. We, on behalf of our client, make the counter offer as follows.

6. As the competition here is very keen, we regret we are unable to accept your prices, which will leave us a very small margin of profit.

7. In view of the above, we suggest that it is to your interest to accept our price and terms of payment as soon as possible.

8. We appreciate your immediate response to our enquiry for plastic flowers.

Key Points of Letters on Making a Counter Offer	Sentences
Thank the offeror for the offer	
Express regret at inability to accept the offer	
State reasons for non-acceptance	
Make a counter offer	
Persuade the offeree to accept the counter offer	

 III. Find the errors in the letter and improve it.

June 2nd, 2022

Dear Sirs,

We are receive of your email dating June 21st, 2022, ask us to offer 100 metric tons of the subject sugar for shipment to Japan and appreciate you interest in our product.

To compliance with your request, we are offering you the following (see the enclose), valid until July 15th.

Please notice that we do not have much in stock. I suggest you accepted our offer as soon as possible.

Yours, sincerely

Ruby

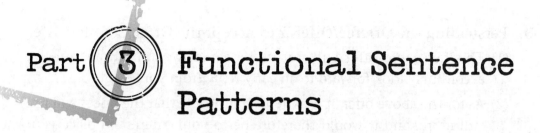

Part ③ Functional Sentence Patterns

1. Confirming Receipt of the Enquiry or Making an Offer

(1) With reference to your enquiry of May 20th, we make you the following offer, which is subject to our final confirmation.

(2) Replying to your enquiry of May 8th, we have the pleasure of quoting our washing machines as follows.

(3) We are in receipt of your enquiry of May 24, and send you samples of our wool yarns, for which we can quote you as follows.

(4) In reply to your enquiry dated June 4th, we take the pleasure of making you the following offer.

(5) We have received your enquiry for 10,000 raincoats on FOB Guangzhou basis.

(6) We have received your enquiry for light-weight raincoats dated May 30th with thanks.

2. Making a Counter Offer with Reasons

(1) As the competition here is very keen, we regret we are unable to accept your prices, which will leave us a very small margin of profit.

(2) As you're well aware that the market is firm, we cannot reduce our price to that level.

(3) We do not see any advantage in your quotation, and would like to know whether you have any better value to offer.

(4) May I suggest that you could perhaps make some allowance on your quoted price that would help to introduce your goods to our customers?

(5) We feel that your quotation is not proper because the price for such material is on the decline at present.

(6) While appreciating your kind offer, we have to say that USD 30 per pair FOB Guangzhou seems to be on the high side.

3. Persuading the Offeree/Offeror to Accept the Offer/Counter Offer

(1) This favorable offer will not be repeated for some time, and we accordingly look forward to an early reply from you.

(2) As for the above offer, it is extremely probable that the prices will rise still more, and it would therefore be to your interest to place your orders as soon as possible.

(3) As the prices quoted are exceptionally low and likely to be adjusted, we would advise you to place orders as soon as possible.

(4) This favorable offer is based on an expanding market and it is competitive.

(5) We think the price we offered you last week is the best one.

(6) If you accept our counter offer, we'll place a trial order with you.

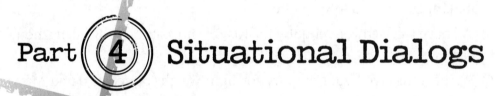

Part 4 Situational Dialogs

Dialog 1: *Mr. Davidson is phoning Miss Zhao, in hopes of getting a favorable offer for refrigerators.*

Davidson: I'm glad you've worked out an offer for us.

Zhao: Well, we're offering 1,000 refrigerators. We will sell them at USD 460 per set CIF European main ports.

Davidson: USD 460 per set? I think the price is rather high. Can you cut the price to, say USD 400 per set?

Zhao: I'm afraid we can't. In consideration of our long-standing business relationship, we are making you our best offer. In the other deals we have done, you know we always gave you the most favorable offer.

Davidson: However, I think your price is a little bit high this time.

Zhao: With this price you'll get good quality goods. The refrigerators we are offering are the most popular model in our company, so I assure you that this is the best offer you can receive.

Davidson: Well, when can you make the shipment?

Zhao: Immediately after we receive your L/C.

Davidson: Okay, for how long will this offer remain valid?

Zhao: It's subject to your reply reaching us on or before June 30th.

Davidson: I'll consider this offer and let you know my decision by then. Thank you very much, Miss Zhao. Bye.

Zhao: Bye.

Dialog 2: *Two days later, Davidson tries to make a counter offer for 1,000 refrigerators on trade terms and price with Miss Zhao on the phone.*

Davidson: Good morning, Miss Zhao. Thank you for your offer for 1,000 refrigerators.

Zhao: You are welcome. Have you made your decision?

Davidson: Not really. I'd like to go over some details with you first. I remember your price is based on CIF European main ports. Can you offer on FOB basis? We have agreements with shipping lines and insurance companies at our end. We can receive good rates from them, so we'd like to arrange shipment and insurance by ourselves.

Zhao: Okay, that's fine, the price should be lower. We offer USD 450 dollars per set FOB Shanghai.

Davidson: I have to say this price is not what I expected. You know, your refrigerators are not as well-known as international famous brands like GE, Siemens, and Electrolux. It'll cost us a lot to promote your products here, and it is really risky for us to do that. I hope you can lower your price by 10%.

Zhao: Our refrigerators are very competitive against the famous brands. They are not so expensive, but they are of the same quality, or maybe even better quality than that of the big brands. People in your place will love them once they find out how well they work.

Davidson: I still think 10% reduction is quite reasonable for all the efforts and risk.

Zhao: I know you make greater efforts to push the sales of our refrigerators and we really appreciate it if you help us to promote our products in your market. When we make this offer, we have considered all the factors. What about a 5% reduction? That's all I can do.

Davidson: Okay, I'll talk to my supervisor and get back to you before June 30th.

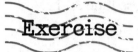

Exercise

Work in pairs and make a business dialog with your partner on making offers according to the information given in the cue cards.

Cue Card A

You are Mr./Ms. Zhang, salesperson of an import company. You need to:

- confirm receipt of the offer;
- regret being unable to accept it because the quoted price is too high;
- ask for price reduction;
- agree with thanks.

Cue Card B

You are Mr./Ms. Prior, the sales manager of an export company. You need to:

- disagree because of a brisk demand;
- suggest meeting each other half way;
- expect a long friendly business relationship in the future.

Part ⑤ Skill Training

I. Match the words and phrases in the left column with their translations in the right column.

1. appreciate   A. 向某人保证某事

2. be out of line with...   B. 与……不符

3. be in a position to do⋯   C. 按照你的要求

4. make an offer for⋯   D. 意识到⋯⋯

5. be subject to⋯   E. 考虑到⋯⋯, 鉴于⋯⋯

6. draw one's attention to⋯   F. 以⋯⋯为条件

7. assure sb. of sth.   G. 感激

8. considering⋯   H. 让某人注意⋯⋯

9. at your request   I. 有能力做⋯⋯

10. be aware of⋯   J. 就⋯⋯报盘

II. Fill in the blanks with appropriate prepositions.

1. Our quotation _____ Tiantan brand shirts is valid for 10 days.

2. The buyer made a bid _____ $2,500 per ton _____ walnut-meat.

3. Green tea, first grade, is at present _____ stock now.

4. We are _____ receipt of your L/C No. 7788 _____ which we thank you very much.

5. _____ compliance _____ your request, we now quote you subject _____ our confirmation _____ the following.

6. We would suggest that you place the order _____ us _____ delay.

7. It's obvious that such a growing demand will result _____ a price increase.

8. _____ all probability, this offer will not be repeated _____ some time, and we accordingly look forward to receiving an early reply _____ you.

9. Please let us know _____ return the lowest price _____ which you can execute this order CIF Boston.

10. As this product has been _____ heavy demand since last year, we strongly recommend that you accept the offer as soon as you can.

III. Choose the best answer to complete each of the following sentences.

1. If you are interested, we will send you a sample lot _____ charge.

A. within   B. for

C. in   D. free of

2. We are making you our quotation for shoes _____.

    A. as follows   B. as following

    C. as follow   D. following

3. We have been _____ with that firm for many years.

    A. making business   B. contacting

    C. dealing   D. supplying

4. We are prepared to keep the offer open _____ 25th this month.

    A. in   B. on

    C. to   D. until

5. We will withdraw the offer if we should not hear _____ you by the end of this week.

    A. of   B. from

    C. by   D. to

6. As our products are of high quality and at moderate price, they _____ fast sales in the international market.

    A. have   B. get

    C. enjoy   D. make

7. Your prompt reply _____.

    A. will be highly appreciated   B. will be thankful

    C. is thanked   D. is appreciated high

8. We assure you that you will find a ready sale _____ this type of new product.

    A. to   B. for

    C. on   D. in

9. We are _____ give such a big discount because of the rising labor cost.

    A. in a position to   B. at a position to

    C. in no position to   D. at no position to

10. Please _____ that your order will be shipped as stipulated in the contract.

    A. assure   B. assured

    C. be sure   D. rest assured

IV. **Translate the following sentences into English or Chinese respectively.**

1. 该报价为最优惠价格，恕不还价。

2. 上述报盘无约束力。

3. 试销订货会使你们相信我们的产品优质。

4. 贵公司 21 日寄来的价目表很完整，但所列付款条件不符合我们的贸易惯例。

5. 兹确认我方已报你方核桃仁 20 吨，每吨 2 500 美元，CIF 伦敦，10 月的船期。

6. Your price is found to be out of line with the prevailing market level.

7. We hope to conclude the business at a price 10% lower than your quotation.

8. For your information, the market is weak with a downward tendency. We suggest your acceptance of our counter offer.

9. We're making you a firm offer as follows, subject to your reply reaching us by the end of this week.

10. We note that these quotations are open for a week only because of the frequent fluctuations of the market price.

V. **Write business letters according to the following situations.**

1. You are Ms. Zhang Lin, a sales manager from Luhu Trading Company in Guangzhou, who is making an offer to Mr. Hamster, after receiving his enquiry for all-cotton tablecloths. You should introduce your products, make an offer and inform him of your usual terms of payment.

2. You are Mr. Hamster, the sales manager at a Canadian import company, who is writing a counter-offer letter to Ms. Zhang Lin, after receiving her offer for all-cotton tablecloths. You would like her to cut down the price by 5% and give your reasons.

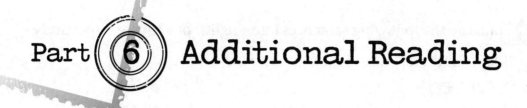

Part 6 Additional Reading

Making Offers in Business Negotiations

Business negotiation is the process in which the seller and the buyer negotiate about the trade terms in order to reach an agreement about the sales of goods.

A business negotiation usually undergoes four stages: enquiry, offer, counter offer, and acceptance. Among them, the offer and the acceptance are indispensable stages, because they're required for the formation of a sales contract.

An offer can be divided into a firm offer and a non-firm offer. In a firm offer, the offeror's intention of making a contract is definitely indicated, and under the firm offer, the offeror cannot revoke or amend what he has offered during the validity of the offer. Generally speaking, there are four requisite conditions that a firm offer must satisfy.

- It must be sent to one or more specific persons.

- The contents of the offer must be definite, that is, the conditions given must be complete, clear, and final. A firm offer should include at least three specific conditions: the name, the quantity, and the price of the commodity.

- It must indicate that once it has been unconditionally accepted by the offeree within the validity, the offer is binding on both parties.

- It takes effect only after the offer reaches the offeree. It's always necessary to state the specific time zone when the offeror specifies the time of arrival.

The non-firm offer is unclear, incomplete, and with reservation; it's not binding on the offeror.

Chapter 5

Acceptance and Orders

Learning Objectives

By completing this unit, students will learn:

- the importance of acceptance and placing orders;
- how to analyze case letters on acceptance and orders;
- useful expressions and sentence patterns related to acceptance and orders;
- how to negotiate on acceptance and orders.

Lead-in

Work in groups, discuss the following questions and then share your answers with the whole class.

1. What does acceptance refer to in international trade?

2. What role does acceptance play in international trade?

3. Do buyers have to sign a contract before accepting the offer?

4. What constituents should be included in a letter on placing or accepting orders?

5. Can the seller decline the buyer's orders after making an acceptance?

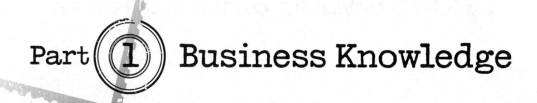

Part ① Business Knowledge

Section 1 Acceptance

Acceptance is the final step of both parties to consent to the terms of the offer. It is common for the terms of the offer to be negotiated before acceptance. While the parties do intend to agree to the final terms of the contract, they could indicate their idea through conduct or communication, then formal acceptance of an offer is not required.

It is also not always necessary that acceptance be in the form of a signature on a piece of paper, although this is the most commonly accepted agreement between parties. For instance, if a party performs an act that would not otherwise happen, such as a painting contractor painting a house, or a professional house-moving company moving furniture from one location to another, it would be interpreted as acceptance and agreement to the terms of the offer.

If one party owns something and another party wishes to use it, and is willing to pay for that right, a contract is the safest way to make sure both parties are protected in the case of something going wrong. No matter how minor or major the exchange is, it all starts with an offer being made and that offer being accepted.

Therefore, it can be concluded that acceptance is the commitment in the law. It refers to the offeree's willingness to sign a contract and full agreement to all the terms of the offer within its validity.

Exercises

I. Match the words and phrases in the left column with their translations in the middle column and definitions in the right column.

1. legally binding   A. 条款   a. to agree to or to give permission

2. terms   B. 有法律约束力的   b. something must be obeyed or carried out because it is accepted in law

3. negotiate   C. 同意   c. the time limit of something being legally or officially acceptable

4. consent to   D. 承诺   d. to arrange for or bring about through conference, discussion, and compromise to agree

5. commitment   E. 有效期   e. the conditions that people offer, demand or accept when they make an agreement or a contract

6. validity   F. 协商   f. a promise to do something

II. Decide whether the statements are true (T) or false (F) according to the passage.

1. Before acceptance, two parties usually negotiate the terms of the offer. (   )

2. Formal acceptance of an offer is absolutely necessary. (   )

3. Two parties should always sign on paper to show the acceptance. (   )

4. A written acceptance is the key step to placing an order. (   )

5. The offeree has to show his agreement to the terms and conditions of the offer within a stipulated time limit if he wants to conclude the deal. (   )

Section 2 Order

An order refers to an oral or written request to supply a specified quantity of goods. It may be the result of an offer or a counter offer with a positive acceptance. It may be given by letters, emails, or faxes, or even orally at a meeting. But order letters are a common form of correspondence for obtaining goods and services.

An order letter must include all the necessary details to make it complete, namely name of goods, catalog No. and sample No.; price of goods, including unit price, total value; quantity of goods; quality requirement, grade, model name; origin and material; weight, dimensions, color, and pattern; packing and marking; terms of payment; delivery requirements, including place, date, mode of transport, whether the order will be carriage paid or to collect, etc.; documents, such as bill of lading, commercial invoices, insurance policy; special features and others, for example, alternatives if exact goods required are not available.

An order should be replied in good time. If the seller accepts it, he or she had better repeat the terms and deliver his or her goodwill in the closing section. Praising that the order is a wise one, and expressing thanks to a long-time customer for his or her repeat patronage and a hearty welcome to a new customer are important. Once accepted, the order will be legally binding and require both parties to honor their agreement. If the seller declines the buyer's order, utmost care should be taken when he or she writes a rejection so as to cause no harm to future business.

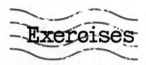

I. Read the passage and finish the mind-map of an order letter.

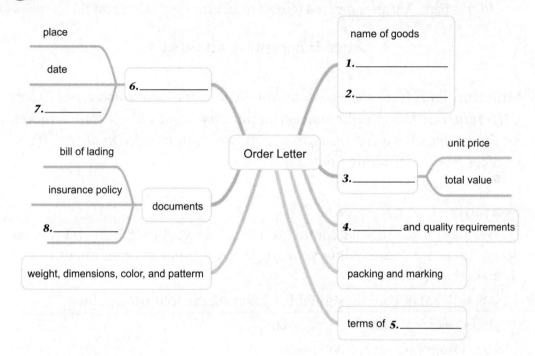

II. Read the passage and answer the following questions.

1. What is the usual way to make the supplier know that the buyer accepts the final offer?

_____

2. What does the supplier usually do when he or she decides to accept the buyer's order?

_____

3. What is the principle of writing an order letter?

_____

4. How will the supplier reply to the order when it is from a new customer?

_____

5. What will the supplier do when he or she decides to decline the buyer's order?

_____

Part ② Case Study

In this part, you are supposed to read four letters on orders and their replies.

Letter 1: Accepting an order

Situation: *Min is a sales assistant from China National Import and Export Corporation. After several rounds of negotiations and careful consideration, he finally makes up his mind to accept the counter offer made by Tycon Outdoor Products Trading Company.*

Dear Jerry,

We have received your counter offer and are glad to inform you that we decide to accept it, including your suggested minimum order quantity and shortened lead time.

We will email you our **signed P/I** covering the following points:

Item: Men's Hoodie Raincoat A205

Minimum quantity: 5,000 pieces

Unit price: USD 5.00 per piece FOB Guangzhou

Packing: 6 dozen to a carton lined with plastic sheet

Lead time: 8 days

Payment: L/C at sight in our favor

Shipment: to be made within 15 days after receipt of the L/C

Please contact us if you have any questions about this order.

Best regards,

Min

Letter 2: Placing an order

Situation: *Johnson, the general manager of Golden Star Electronics Co. Ltd. from Britain, has examined the quality of samples, and finally accepted the quotation and now he is writing a letter to place an order.*

Dear Wen,

Thank you for your samples, along with the quotation for your washing machines of June 4th.

We have examined the samples you sent on June 4th. We found the quality of these washing machines up to our requirement and we are delighted to inform you that we decide to place an order for 850 sets of washing machines with you at the price and terms mentioned in your quotation, and we desire to call your immediate and best attention to our order.

All these products are urgently required by our customers. We, therefore, hope you will **arrange the shipment** ASAP. We shall **be obliged** if you will kindly let us have the **shipping advice** at your earliest convenience after you effect shipment.

If this first order proves satisfactory, we shall be happy to place substantial orders with you.

Waiting for your early reply.

Yours faithfully,

Johnson

Letter 3: Accepting an order

Situation: *In reply to Johnson's order letter, Wen, a sales manager from Guangdong Electric Import and Export Co. Ltd., informs that his order has been accepted and the shipping advice will be sent once the goods have been shipped.*

Dear Johnson,

Thank you very much for your kind order for our washing machines which we have accepted, and you may rely on us to give your orders prompt attention.

You may **rest assured** that the washing machines under order No. 123 would be carefully packed to prevent damage **in transit**. We shall send you the shipping advice and the invoice once the goods have been shipped.

Since our machines are excellent in quality, we are sure you will be pleased to collect good comments about these goods from your consumers, and build up a market for the products in your country.

We hope this will lead to more **considerable orders**.

Yours faithfully,

Wen

Letter 4: Declining the order

Situation: *In reply to Benny's order letter, Daniel, a sales manager from a Chinese export company, regrettably informs that her order has been declined due to some reasons.*

Dear Benny,

We thank you very much for your order of June 3rd. After careful consideration on your request, however, we have come to the conclusion that we have to **decline the said order**.

The handbags in fact have been the best-seller for the last few months, but the sales now are going down fast, so we have stopped producing this item since last week. And unfortunately to tell you, it is out of stock in our warehouse. So, it would not be possible to restart to produce 10,000 pieces of these handbags within 20 days without interrupting our normal production as we **are** already **heavily committed**.

We regret not being in a position to accept your order, or could you take the **substitutes**? Or could you wait for a longer lead time? Please let us have any other enquiries of yours, as we shall be too pleased to meet your requirements.

Awaiting your reply keenly.

Yours truly,

Daniel

Words and Expressions

1. signed P/I (Proforma Invoice) 已签署的形式发票
2. arrange the shipment 安排运输
3. be obliged 不胜感激
4. shipping advice 装运通知
5. rest assured 放心，确信无误
6. in transit 运输途中
7. considerable order 大量订单
8. decline the said order 拒绝该订单
9. be heavily committed 订单太多
10. substitute *n.* 替代品

Exercises

I. Match the sentences with the key points of letters on placing or accepting orders and finish the table below.

1. Thank you for your quotation of July 10th, 2022.
2. And as you have promised, your delivery will reach not later than March 26th, 2022.
3. We have decided to place a trial order with you on the following items at the price and terms we have both agreed on.
4. We want to make it clear that the total order quantity should be shipped before July.
5. We are delighted to inform you that we accept your 5% discount and decide to place a trial order for your products as follows.
6. Thank you for your speedy samples, along with the quotation for your washing machines of June 4th.

Key Points of Letters on Placing or Accepting Orders	Sentences
Thank for the offer/quotation	
Make a decision to place an order	
Confirm the terms and conditions	

II. Find the errors in the letter and improve it.

June 13th, 2022

Dear Haier Company,

I am Johnson. I am the Purchase Manager. We are delight to inform you that we have accepted your offer and decided to place a trial order as agreed.

We need 100 sets of products and each one is US $805, so the total number is US $80,500. The delivery should reach us before June 30th, 2022. As all these products urgently required by our customers, any delay in shipment will lead to withdraw.

Yours faithfully,

Johnson

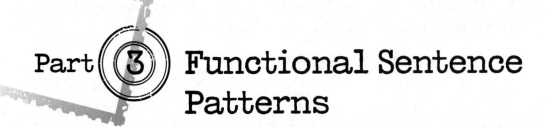

Part 3 Functional Sentence Patterns

1. Accepting an Offer / a Counter Offer

(1) We have received your samples and we are glad to inform you that we decide to accept your revised offer.

(2) Taking the quality into consideration, we accept your offer.

(3) We are glad to inform you that we have accepted your counter offer dated January 25th for TV sets.

(4) We are pleased to accept your offer of June 15th as we are satisfied with your price as well as the time of shipment.

(5) We have accepted your counter offer by email for 850 sets of washing machines at USD 520 per set FOB Guangzhou.

2. **Placing an Order**

(1) We are pleased to place with you an order for 3,000 computers in current stock at the prices you quoted.

(2) We are delighted to inform you that we accept your 5% discount and decide to place a trial order for your products.

(3) We find both price and quality of your products satisfactory to our clients and we are pleased to give you an order for the items on this sheet.

(4) Thank you for your email of May 24th enclosing your latest illustrated catalog. We would like to order 1,200 sets of color TV.

(5) This is a trial order. If the quality proves to be satisfactory, we will give you larger orders in the future.

3. **Confirming Terms/Orders**

(1) Let's discuss the clauses to see if we agree on all the terms.

(2) Referring to the emails exchanged between us recently, we confirm the following order placed with you.

(3) Let's go through the details of your order.

(4) We are pleased to confirm your order of June 1st for 850 sets of washing machines.

(5) We acknowledge with thanks your order of May 24th for 1,000 pieces of raincoats.

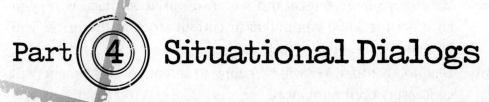

Part ④ Situational Dialogs

Dialog 1: *Fobert and Jan have negotiated over the price of T-shirt with each other for nearly one month. Now Fobert asks for a 5% discount. Though Jan disagrees with him, he makes a concession too. Finally, they iron out all the details.*

Fobert: Good morning. Let's revert to our negotiation.

Jan: OK, Fobert. That's great.

Fobert: I've told our manager about what we've negotiated. And our company insists a 5% discount.

Jan: Well, it will leave us a very little margin of profit.

Fobert: Jan, we need to hammer something out today. If I go back empty-handed, I might be coming back to you soon to ask for a job.

Jan: OK, let's meet each other half way, say, 3% discount off. It's the best we can do.

Fobert: Good, thanks. Let's iron out all the details. The price is USD 4.5/pc CIF New York. And when can you effect shipment?

Jan: We can make shipment by May 31st.

Fobert: And the terms of payment?

Jan: Right. Our usual terms of payment are made by confirmed and irrevocable L/C.

Fobert: Got it. We will apply for issuing L/C not later than April 15th.

Jan: I can agree to that. Well, if there's nothing else, I think we've settled everything.

Fobert: Jan, this deal promises big returns for both sides. If we find both price and quality of your products satisfactory to our clients, we will place a further order with you in the future.

Dialog 2: *Rebecca, the salesperson from an import company, is interested in the goods and intends to place an order with Jenny, the salesperson from an export company. Now they are talking with each other on the details of the order.*

Rebecca: We like your products, and we are pleased to place with you an order for 3,000 computers in current stock at the prices you quoted.

Jenny: Glad to hear that! We will be happy to accept your order, and will get to work on it right away.

Rebecca: We will send you a purchase order soon. We want to ask you to speed up the execution of the order.

Jenny: I don't think that will be a problem, please rest assured. We will carry out the order when the purchase order gets here.

Rebecca: Great. This is our initial order; we hope that everything will go well.

Jenny: Thank you very much for your trial order, and we hope it will lead to further business between us. If there is any further information you require, please contact us.

Rebecca: Thanks a lot. We will email our purchase order to you within two days.

Jenny: OK, and you are kindly requested to open the L/C as soon as possible.

Rebecca: Of course. We will execute the order as stipulated.

Jenny: Thanks, we promise to make shipment as soon as possible.

Exercise

Work in pairs and make a business dialog with your partner on acceptance and placing orders according to the information given in the cue cards.

Cue Card A

> You are Mr./Ms. Biterlif, the manager of an import company. You need to:
> - extend your greetings and intention of placing an order with the seller;
> - confirm some of the terms and conditions like terms of payment, date of shipment, insurance, etc.;
> - show your expectation to get the goods in time;
> - show thanks for the cooperative spirit.

Cue Card B

> You are Mr./Ms. Yan, sales manager from an export company. You need to:
> - greet your partner and show your thanks;
> - confirm the information as required;
> - promise to execute the order as stipulated;
> - express goodwill.

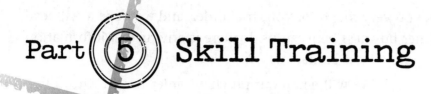

Part ⑤ Skill Training

I. Match the words and phrases in the left column with their translations in the right column.

1.	substitute	A.	大量订单
2.	considerable order	B.	履行订单
3.	in stock	C.	有存货
4.	execute the order	D.	拒绝订单
5.	decline the order	E.	替代品
6.	lead time	F.	首笔订单
7.	initial order	G.	订购单 / 购买单
8.	purchase order	H.	生产周期
9.	margin of profit	I.	装运期
10.	time of shipment	J.	利润空间

II. Fill in the blanks with appropriate words or phrases given in the box.

inform	payment	total amount	article
quotation	quantity	place an order	unit price
quality	delivery date		

Dear Sirs,

Thank you for your **1.** _____ on June 10th, 2022. We are delighted to **2.** _____ you that we accept your 5% discount and decide to **3.** _____ with you at the prices and terms we have both agreed on.

    4. _____ : Changhong air conditioner

    5. _____ : Exactly the same as per samples

6. _____ : 100 sets

7. _____ : US $ 805 per set FOB Guangzhou

8. _____ : US $ 80,500

9. _____ : Arrive before August 30th, 2022

10. _____ : Draft at 30 d/s under an irrevocable L/C

Sincerely yours,

Billy

III. **Translate the following sentences into English or Chinese respectively.**

1. 我们希望这将带来更多可观的订单。

2. 订单现已完成并发往大连码头等待装船。

3. 据我们最近交换的电子邮件，我们确认向您下了以下订单。

4. 仔细考虑您的请求后，我们不得不拒绝上述订单。

5. 我们已接受你方有关 850 台洗衣机的电邮还盘，每台 520 美元，FOB 广州。

6. Please don't forget that bank details should be marked in the P/I for us to open the L/C.

7. We are pleased to place an order with you for 3,000 computers in current stock at the prices you quoted.

8. We have received your samples and are glad to inform you that we decide to accept your revised offer, including your suggested terms of payment.

9. If the order is not executed within the stipulated time, we shall have to cancel it.

10. Please open an L/C in favor of ABC Company before shipping.

IV. **Write a business letter according to the following situation.**

After receiving samples, ABC Trading Company decided to place their first order with Tianjin Textiles Corporation. The following are the items they are going to order based on the agreed quotation: (1) 5,000 yards of F82 cotton cloth at $ 21.00 per yard; (2) 2,000 yards of F85 cotton cloth at $ 22.00 per yard; (3) 2,000 yards of F86 cotton cloth at $ 25.00 per yard.

You should include time of delivery in the letter and agree to all other conditions as per the quotation.

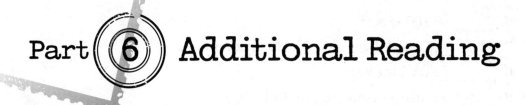

Part 6 Additional Reading

How to Decline a Customer's Purchase Order

Small business owners pray for purchase orders (PO), but sometimes problems come with those POs. Since accepting a purchase order creates a legal contract to deliver goods, sometimes the best thing to do is to decline the order. How you go about declining the PO depends on whether you want to keep the customer or would rather discourage further dealings. In any case, a polite response avoids further problems and can increase customer loyalty. Here are some problems and effective solutions listed below.

1. Problems with Payment

A new customer might write a 90-day payment into a purchase order. If you only grant 30-day payment terms, simply send a quick note to the customer thanking him or her for the order and explaining that your payment terms require payment in full within 30 days. Ask for a corrected PO. This leaves the decision to cancel the order up to the customer and leaves the door open to negotiation that might retain the customer under a shorter payment schedule acceptable to you.

2. Problems with Delivery

Sometimes you receive a PO for a product that you no longer carry or in a number that you can't supply from your current stock. If you no longer carry the product, explain this and suggest alternative products that you do carry. If you don't have enough stock to fill the order, but can supply the total number of units in separate deliveries over time, indicate a proposed delivery schedule. Again, this gives your customer the option of canceling the order and implies that you are a trustworthy source who won't promise something you can't deliver.

3. Potential Fraud

Never accept a PO that contains inconsistencies with a customer's history or that has unusual terms without first confirming it with the customer.

It might be a fraudulent PO or a mistake. A quick phone call or email will reveal whether the PO is valid and give you an opportunity to negotiate any requested terms with which you disagree.

4. Difficult Customer

An outright decline of a PO should be avoided if there is a way to politely suggest alternative terms or negotiate details. However, when a problem customer who usually ends up costing you money sends in an order, and you want to avoid doing business with that customer, reply with a polite note attached to the PO stating that you are unable to fill the order at this time and must decline. The less said, the better; avoid stating negatives such as poor payment history or bad customer behavior. Eventually, your difficult customer will find another supplier.

Chapter 6

Contracts

Learning Objectives

By completing this unit, students will learn:

- contracts in international business and format of contracts;
- how to analyze case letters on contracts;
- useful expressions and sentence patterns related to signing a contract;
- how to negotiate on terms of a contract.

Lead-in

Work in groups, discuss the following questions and then share your answers with the whole class.

1. How important is it to sign a contract in international trade?

2. What information should be included in a contract?

3. What are the forms of written contract forms?

4. What constituents should be included in a letter on contracts?

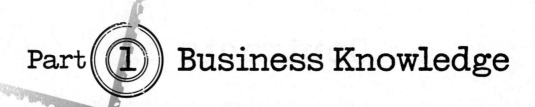

Part ① Business Knowledge

Section 1 Contracts in Business

At one time, transacting business was easy. Two people agreed to make a trade, and both parties honored their words. But in the 21st century, professionals are all too aware of the long history of deal-breaking and lawsuits that have taken place all around them. In business, contracts are important because they outline expectations for both parties, protect both parties if those expectations aren't met and lock in the price that will be paid for services.

A contract is a written agreement between two parties that details the terms of a transaction. In a business, it generally states the work that will be performed, along with important information like due dates and costs.

It can be easy to make your contract far longer and more complicated than it needs to be, but it's best for everyone to try to keep it simple. Still, your business contract should at least include the following:

- General timeline or, if possible, exact due dates for each milestone. Nothing that you discussed should be left out of the contract if you want it to be enforceable.

- Payment amounts and terms. How many days will the person have after delivery to remit that payment, and how will it be made?

- The circumstances under which the contract can be terminated and how that will be handled. If dispute mediation becomes necessary, the contract should also outline how that will take place.

- A non-compete or non-disclosure clause if one or both parties may feel it necessary to be included.

- Any terms related to failed obligations. If, for instance, payment isn't remitted by a certain date, the contract should outline how much late payment fee will be paid.

If you can afford an attorney, it would be wise to have one look over your contract to make sure you've covered everything. Once you have the initial draft, you should be able to simply update it with all of your clients.

Hopefully, you'll never have to take legal action based on the contract, which means the project will end and you'll move on to the next project. Both parties should keep a copy of the contract on file for several years in case a later issue should arise. You'll also have the template that you can adjust based on the lessons you've learned from previous projects.

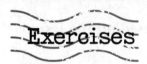
Exercises

I. Read the passage and choose the best answer to each question.

1. Which of the following statements is NOT about the importance of contracts?

A. They outline expectations for both parties.

B. Transacting business is easy.

C. They lock in the price that will be paid for services.

D. They protect both parties if those expectations aren't met.

2. In a business, a contract generally states the following EXCEPT _____.

A. general timeline

B. payment amounts and terms

C. any terms related to failed obligations

D. the factory of the goods

3. Which of the following should be outlined in a contract if payment isn't remitted by a certain date?

A. The latest shipment date.

B. The contract will be void immediately.

C. Both parties will never do business again.

D. How much late payment fee will be paid?

4. If dispute mediation becomes necessary, a contract should also outline the following EXCEPT _____.

A. how that will take place

B. the circumstances under which the contract can be terminated

C. how that will be handled

D. which attorney will be employed

5. When you have to take legal action based on the contract, it means the following EXCEPT _____.

A. the project will end

B. you'll move on to the next project

C. a later issue should arise

D. you'll have the template that you can adjust based on the lessons you've learned from previous projects

II. Decide whether the statements are true (T) or false (F) according to the passage.

1. A contract is a written agreement between two parties that details the terms of a transaction. (   )

2. It's better to make your contract long and complicated than it needs to be. (   )

3. Something that you discussed should be left out of the contract if you want it to be enforceable. (   )

4. If you can afford an attorney, it would be wise to have one look over your contract. (   )

5. Both parties should throw the copy of the contract away since the contract has been executed. (   )

Section 2 Format and Main Contents of a Contract or Confirmation

There are mainly four written forms of the business contract in import and export business, i.e., contract, confirmation, agreement, and memorandum, among which the former two are the most commonly used. Both the sales contract and the sales confirmation have the same legal effect. The main differences lie in the fact that the contract is comparatively more formal and detailed, while the confirmation covers only the essential terms and conditions in a transaction.

A contract should be accurate and precise, and is usually in set forms. Although its specific contents may vary with different situations, a formal written sales contract or confirmation generally includes the three parts: head, body, and end.

The head is the beginning of the contract which usually consists of contract title, contract number, date and place of signing the contract, names and addresses of both parties and preface. As for the body, it is the most important message of a contract, reflecting duties and obligations of both parties. It can be further divided into essential terms and conditions and general ones. The essential terms and conditions must be included in a contract, including name of commodity and specification, quality, quantity, price, packing, insurance, shipment, and terms of payment while the general ones belong to optional parts, e.g., inspection, claims, force majeure, arbitration and so on, and are often used between new trade partners. The end indicates the number of original copies of the contract, the language used, the law applied, signature and seal.

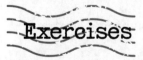

Exercises

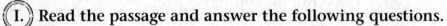

I. **Read the passage and answer the following questions.**

1. Which two are the most commonly used written forms of the business contract in import and export business?

   _____

2. What are the differences between the sales contract and the sales confirmation?

   _____

3. How many parts are generally included in a formal written sales contract or confirmation? What are they?

_____

4. What is the most important message of a contract?

_____

5. What are the essential terms and conditions in a contract?

_____

II. **Decide whether the statements are true (T) or false (F) according to the passage.**

1. The sales contract and the sales confirmation have different legal effects. (   )

2. A contract should be accurate and precise, and is usually in fixed forms. (   )

3. Duties and obligations of both parties can be reflected in the head of a contract. (   )

4. The general terms of the body is often used between regular trade partners. (   )

5. The signature and seal can be found at the end of a contract. (   )

Part ② Case Study

In this part, you are supposed to read four letters on signing a contract.

Letter 1: Asking for countersigning S/C

Situation: _Shenzhen Jingben Appliance Co. Ltd. accepts the counter offer of Canada Aston Company for 3,000 TV sets, and asks Aston Company to countersign the sales contract enclosed in the letter._

Dear Mr. Braden,

We are pleased that our business deal for 3,000 TV sets has gone well so far. At present, we are sending you a **scanned copy** of the **sales contract** No. JN053 **in duplicate** after being signed by our president. Please check the **attachment**, one copy of which please **countersign** and return to us **for our file**.

You may rest assured that we will **fulfill the order** in strict accordance with the stipulations of the contract with the least possible delay upon receipt of the duly-countersigned contract.

Hope to receive more enquiries and orders from you. We are always at your service.

Best regards.

Yours,

Zhou Hu

Letter 2: Returning countersigned contracts

Situation: *In reply to Zhou Hu, Canada Aston Company writes an email to Shenzhen Jingben Appliance Co. Ltd. by returning the countersigned contracts and expecting further orders.*

Dear Mr. Hu,

We confirm that we have received the sales contract No. JN053 for 3,000 TV sets from your company. We have countersigned the contract as required and sent back the scanned copy of the contract by email.

We have opened the relevant L/C **in your favor** and it will reach you on time. Please check the goods carefully and arrange shipment after receiving the said L/C. We need your **special attention to** this.

As for the additional quantity, we hope you can give us your quotation as soon as possible. We are now considering placing an order for another 1,500 sets.

I hope this transaction will **pave the way for** future cooperation between us.

Looking forward to your early reply.

Yours sincerely,

Braden

Letter 3: Asking for revising the contract

Situation: *After receiving the draft contract, INCD Import and Export Co. Ltd. examined it carefully and found that there were some discrepancies compared with the terms previously reached with Wanli Group Co. Ltd., so they write to ask Wanli to revise the contract as soon as possible.*

Dear Ms. Lee,

Thanks for your great efforts in speeding up the execution of this order.

Immediately after receiving the draft contract, we checked it carefully and thoroughly. We absolutely admire the good job you've done in the process, but inevitably there are still details that need further discussion and revision. Delivery time should be clearer. It should be amended to read as follows: "Not later than July 10th, 2022". Furthermore, "**transshipment** not allowed, **partial shipment** not allowed" should be added in the **provision**, while other terms remain the same.

It is highly appreciated to revise the contract and send it back to me for signature as soon as possible. We are waiting for your confirmation.

Best regards.

Yours faithfully,

Jennifer

Letter 4: Confirming the terms in the contract

Situation: *In reply to Jennifer's request for revising some terms in the contract, Lucy Lee, the general manager from Wanli Group Co. Ltd., writes a letter to confirm the terms and sends the revised sales contract for signature.*

Dear Jennifer,

Your letter of June 13th asking us to revise some terms in the contract has been received with thanks.

As for your proposal to make the delivery time clearer, it is acceptable to amend it to "Not later than July 10th, 2022". With regard to shipment, it is our usual practice to make shipment with transshipment not allowed and partial shipment allowed. However, in view of the long and friendly relationship between us, we are willing to make an exception for you this time and add your request for shipment in the provision. However, it should be noted that this **departure from our usual practice** is only for this transaction.

We will soon email you our revised S/C No. 208, and please send it back duly countersigned.

We look forward to further **expansion** of trade to our **mutual benefit**.

Best,

Lucy Lee

Words and Expressions

1. scanned copy 扫描件

2. sales contract 销售合同，简称为 S/C

3. in duplicate 一式两份

4. attachment *n.* 附件

5. countersign *v.* 会签，连署

6. for one's file/record (s) 供……存档

7. fulfill/execute the order 履行订单

8. in your favor 以你方为受益人

9. special attention to... 特别关注……

10. pave the way for... 为……铺平道路

11. transshipment *n.* 转运

12. partial shipment 分批装运

13. provision *n.* 规定；条款

14. departure from one's usual practice 违背某人的惯例

15. expansion *n.* 扩大

16. mutual benefit 共同利益，互利

Exercises

I. **Match the sentences with the key points of letters on contracts and finish the table below.**

1. As requested in the contract, we are going to effect shipment before September 10th.

2. We are pleased to send S/C No. 2060 in duplicate, one copy of which please countersign and return to us for our file.

3. We agreed to conclude the transaction at the price of USD 500 per ton.

4. I hope this transaction will pave the way for future cooperation between us.

5. It is hoped that you will speed up the opening of your L/C so as to fulfill the terms of the contract.

Key Points of Letters on Contracts	Sentences
Confirm the order	
Request for countersigning the contract	
Hope to open the L/C soon	
Ensure prompt shipment	
Expect further cooperation	

II. **Match the sentences with the key points of letters on replying to signing a contract and finish the table below.**

1. We have instructed the bank of Tokyo to open the relevant L/C in your favor, and it will reach you soon.

2. We must reiterate that the coffee makers have to be delivered on or before July 2nd due to commitments we have made to our customers.

3. In reply to your email dated January 26th, 2022, we are happy to confirm your order for 5,000 sets of microwave ovens.

4. As for the additional quantity, we hope you can give us your quotation as soon as possible.

5. We have countersigned the contract as required and sent back the scanned copy of the contract.

Key Points of Letters on Replying to Signing a Contract	Sentences
Confirm the order	
Inform the counter signature as requested	
Ensure the opening of the L/C	
Ask for prompt shipment	
Invite additional orders	

 III. Find the errors in the letter and improve it.

June 18th, 2022

Dear Sirs,

We have booked your order for bed sheets and pillow cases and are sending you our sales confirmation. Please sign and return one copy to us.

It is understood that a letter of credit in your favor covering the above-mentioned goods will be established immediately. We wish to point out that the stipulations in the relevant credit should not violate the terms stated in our amendments. You may rest assured that we shall effect shipment.

We appreciate if you cooperate and look forward to receiving your further orders.

Yours faithfully,

Eric

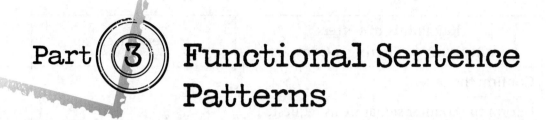

Part ③ Functional Sentence Patterns

1. Recalling the Satisfactory Transaction

(1) We are glad to have concluded business with you in the captioned goods.

(2) In reply to your email dated January 26, we are happy to confirm your order for 5,000 sets of microwave ovens.

(3) We are glad that through our mutual effort, finally we have reached the agreement.

(4) We thank you for your quotation of February 20th and enclose our Purchase Order No. 456 for the captioned goods.

(5) Through your full cooperation, we are able to place our trial order at your revised price.

2. Asking for Counter Signature

(1) You are required to sign the sales conformation and email it back for our file at your earliest convenience.

(2) We are sending you the scanned copy of our Sales Contract No. DY351. Please countersign and return one copy for our file.

(3) Attached is our Sales Contract No. 102 covering the above order, please countersign it.

(4) Please return to us one of them by fax, completed with your signature.

(5) If you find the contents therein agreeable, please fax it back to us with your company chop.

3. Making Promise to Execute the Contract

(1) Many thanks for giving us a trial order, and we promise that your order will be dealt with promptly and carefully.

(2) We assure you that we will open the relevant L/C through Bank of China in your favor without delay.

(3) In order to promote our friendly relationship, we assure you of our full cooperation in starting business between us early.

(4) Please rest assured that L/C terms would be in exact accordance with the stipulations in our S/C.

(5) We will open the covering L/C in accordance with the terms and conditions laid down in the said S/C.

4. **Expecting Further Cooperation**

(1) We believe the first transaction will turn out to be profitable to both of us.

(2) Thank you for your cooperation, and we are expecting your future orders.

(3) We hope our cooperation in this first order will lead to a brighter future of our business relationship.

(4) If the quality of your products proves to be satisfactory to us, we will place large orders with you in the future.

(5) We believe that the current small business will lead to a series of larger dealings in the near future.

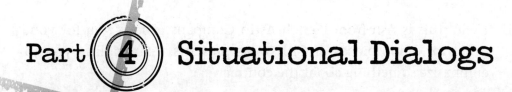

Part ④ Situational Dialogs

Dialog 1: *Guangzhou Hileng Home Appliance Co. Ltd. decided to sign the contract with French Astin Company for 3,600 pieces of Christmas presents.*

Leng: We are glad that through our mutual efforts, finally we have reached the agreement. And now we decide to sign the contract with you for 3,600 pieces of Christmas presents.

Asli: Good. We are glad to conclude business with you. Please go over the draft of the contract.

Leng: OK. Take a seat, please. What would you like, Chinese tea or coffee?

Asli: Thank you. I'd very much like to have a cup of Chinese tea.

Leng: Here you are.

Asli: Finished?

Leng: Yes. I have one question about the date of shipment. We'd like to get the goods ready by the end of November. You see, December is the peak season for Christmas presents. It is important for us to catch it.

Asli: I see. Please rest assured. We'll deliver the goods as soon as we receive your L/C.

Leng: OK, we'll expedite the establishment of L/C.

Asli: Are all the other terms here to your satisfaction?

Leng: Yes, well, if there's nothing else, I think we've settled everything. Can we sign the contract now?

Asli: Sure. Here is the pen.

Leng: I've signed the contract, and please countersign it here.

Asli: Here it is. I think this deal promises big returns for both sides. Let's hope it's the beginning of a long and prosperous relationship.

Dialog 2: *Guangzhou Hileng Home Appliance Co. Ltd. has signed a contract with French Astin Company for 3,600 pieces of Christmas presents. A few days later, the salesman of each company made a telephone call to talk about the execution of the contract.*

Asli: Hello, this is Asli from French Astin Company. Thank you for your order for 3,600 pieces of Christmas presents. I am calling you to emphasize something about the contract.

Leng: OK, go ahead.

Asli: Please see to it that L/C terms should be in exact accordance with the stipulations in our S/C.

Leng: Certainly, we assure you that we'd pay our best attention to it, and open the necessary L/C at an early date.

Asli: Thanks, we will ship the goods without failure as early as possible.

Leng: Emm, we hope that the contract will be fulfilled smoothly and successfully.

Asli: Me, too. And we promise that your order will be dealt with promptly and carefully.

Leng: If the quality of your products proves to be satisfactory to us, we will place large orders with you in the future.

Asli: I am glad to hear that. We sincerely hope to establish a long-term cooperation with you and to get our business developed.

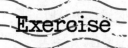

Exercise

Work in pairs and make a business dialog with your partner on a contract according to the information given in the cue cards.

Cue Card A

> You are Mr./Ms. Liezy, the salesperson of an export company. You need to:
> - recall the satisfactory transaction and ask for counter signature;
> - show appreciation for the cooperation;
> - promise to execute the contract strictly in accordance with it;
> - promise to make shipment upon receipt of L/C.

Cue Card B

> You are Mr./Ms. Domet, the salesperson of an import company. You need to:
> - show thanks and agree to countersign the contract and return one copy;
> - expect a smooth execution of this transaction;
> - promise to issue L/C the soonest possible;
> - expect more business in the future.

Part ⑤ Skill Training

I. Match the words and phrases in the left column with their translations in the right column.

1. conclude a transaction with sb.   A. 销售合同条款

2. countersign   B. 供……存档

3.	the scanned copy	C. 符合
4.	for one's file	D. 以你方为受益人
5.	execute the order	E. 在适当的时候；按时地
6.	conform to	F. 与某人达成交易
7.	S/C stipulations	G. 履行订单
8.	in your favor	H. 会签
9.	at your end	I. 扫描件
10.	duly	J. 在你处

II. Fill in the blanks with appropriate words given in the box.

disagreement	communicate	reply	for
conditions	place	via	countersign

Dear Mr. Okada,

Thank you for your cooperation, and finally we decide to **1.** _____ an order with you for 2,000 pieces of smart toys.

In the attachment, please see our Purchase Contract. If you have any **2.** _____ with the terms and **3.** _____ of the Purchase Contract made out by us, please **4.** _____ with me **5.** _____ email or phone call.

If there is no problem with the Purchase Contract, please **6.** _____ it and send one scanned copy back to us **7.** _____ our file. I am anticipating your early **8.** _____.

Yours sincerely,

Alice Chen

III. Choose the best answer to complete each of the following sentences.

1. We hope you can give prompt attention to our request for the _____ of the relative L/C.

A. establishing   B. establish

C. establishment   D. established

2. Referring to the latest exchange of letters, we are pleased to confirm _____ with you a transaction of 100 tons of coal.

A. conclude   B. conclusion

C. to conclude   D. having concluded

3. Thank you for your repeat order which is receiving our immediate attention. As _____, we will effect the shipment well in time.

A. advised   B. referred

C. requested   D. concluded

4. We have made out and sent you our Sales Confirmation No. 6060 _____ and would you send back one copy duly countersigned?

A. in duplicate   B. of duplicate

C. of two copies   D. in two copy

5. We will _____ you of the time of delivery as soon as we make preparation.

A. mention   B. note

C. learn   D. advise

6. In order to ensure the requested shipment, please open the covering L/C _____ should reach us 30 days prior to the date of delivery.

A. which   B. in which

C. on which   D. of which

7. For your information, we have recently _____ with a Japanese exporter a transaction of $10,000 on the terms of D/P at sight.

A. concluded   B. brought

C. realized   D. come to

8. _____ our order of June 17, we will keep you well advised of the relative development.

A. With reference on   B. Regards to

C. Regards on   D. With reference to

9. We return herewith one copy _____ signed to you for your file.

A. with   B. being

C. duly   D. due

10. Since this _____ is concluded successfully, he is obliged to give up the idea of breaking it.

    A. purchase   B. transaction

    C. order   D. contract

IV. Translate the following sentences into English or Chinese respectively.

1. 我们很高兴已经达成 1 000 箱玩具的交易。

2. 请务必按计划发货。

3. 如果第一批货令人满意，我们将再次订货。

4. 请立即开立信用证，以便我们安排装运。

5. 根据我方第 84532 号合同的规定，贵方应在 9 月底前开立相关信用证。

6. The conclusion of this transaction will mark the beginning of our long friendly business relations.

7. We inform you that we'll execute the order duly.

8. It is understood that a letter of credit in our favor covering the above-mentioned goods will be established immediately.

9. We could manage to arrange the shipment in August subject to your L/C reaching here not later than July 15.

10. It should be noted that this departure from our usual practice is only for this transaction.

V. Write a business letter according to the following situation.

Guangzhou Lantian Fabric Co. Ltd. is going to send a sales contract on bed sheets and pillow cases to Brazil Mancim Company for counter signature, indicating that the L/C should be opened promptly and in strict conformity with the terms stated in the amendments, and promising immediate shipment after receiving the L/C.

Part ⑥ Additional Reading

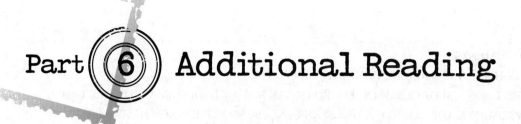

SALES CONTRACT

SELLER: ABC TRADING CORP.   **NO.:** EXP9988

NO.10 BAJING ROAD, BEIJING, CHINA   **DATE:** JAN.10TH, 2022

BUYER: XYZ TRADING CORP.

PLACE: RM909VX BUILDING, LONDON, ENGLAND

THIS CONTRACT IS MADE BY AND AGREED BETWEEN THE BUYER AND SELLER, IN ACCORDANCE WITH THE TERMS AND CONDITIONS STIPULATED BELOW.

COMMODITY & SPECIFICATION	QUANTITY	UNIT PRICE & TRADE TERMS	AMOUNT
SILK T-SHIRT STYLE NO. UE123 AS PER THE ORDER NO. 2022 UE123		CIFC5 LONDON	
COLOUR: TOMATO	2,000 PCS	GBP 15.00/PC	GBP 30,000.00
SILVER	2,000 PCS	GBP 15.00/PC	GBP 30,000.00
SNOW	2,000 PCS	GBP 15.00/PC	GBP 30,000.00
MAROON	2,000 PCS	GBP 15.00/PC	GBP 30,000.00
TOTAL:	8,000 PCS		GBP 120,000.00

TOTAL VALUE	SAY GB POUNDS ONE HUNDRED AND TWENTY THOUSAND ONLY
PACKING	40 PCS ARE PACKED IN ONE EXPORT STANDARD CARTON
TIME OF SHIPMENT	BEFORE APR. 30TH, 2022
PARTIAL SHIPMENT: NOT ALLOWED	TRANSSHIPMENT: ALLOWED
PORT OF LOADING & DESTINATION	FROM TIANJIN CHINA TO LONDON ENGLAND
INSURANCE	TO BE EFFECTED BY THE SELLER FOR 110% INVOICE VALUE COVERING ICC(A) AND WAR RISK
TERMS OF PAYMENT	BY L/C AT 30 DAYS AFTER SIGHT, REACHING THE SELLER BEFORE FEB.15TH, 2022, AND REMAINING VALID FOR NEGOTIATION IN CHINA FOR FURTHER 15 DAYS AFTER THE EFFECTED SHIPMENT. L/C MUST MENTION THIS CONTRACT NUMBER. ALL BANKING CHARGES OUTSIDE CHINA ARE FOR ACCOUNT OF THE DRAWEE.

(Continued)

DOCUMENTS:

+ SIGNED COMMERCIAL INVOICE IN TRIPLICATE.

+ FULL SET (3/3) OF CLEAN ON BOARD OCEAN BILL OF LADING MARKED "FREIGHT PREPAID" MADE OUT TO ORDER BLANK ENDORSED NOTIFYING THE APPLICANT.

+ INSURANCE POLICY IN DUPLICATE ENDORSED IN BLANK.

+ PACKING LIST IN TRIPLICATE.

+ CERTIFICATE OF ORIGIN ISSUED BY CHINA CHAMBER OF COMMERCE

THE SELLER	THE BUYER
ABC TRADING CORP.	XYZ TRADING CORP.
Mike Taylor	Jack Wilson

Chapter 7

Payment

Learning Objectives

By completing this unit, students will learn:

- modes of payment and circulation process of documentary L/C;
- how to analyze case letters on terms of payment;
- useful expressions and sentence patterns related to terms of payment;
- how to negotiate on terms of payment.

Lead-in

Work in groups, discuss the following questions and then share your answers with the whole class.

1. What are the three major modes of payment in international trade?

2. What is the most frequently used mode of payment in international trade?

3. If the buyer doesn't issue an L/C on time, what shall the seller do?

4. What constituents should be included in a letter on terms of payment?

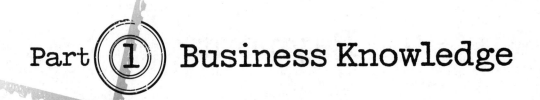

Part ① Business Knowledge

Section 1 Modes of Payment

Payment is an indispensable and complicated part in the course of international trade. The final goal of all business activities should be to recover the goods supplied or services provided. Otherwise, all of them will be meaningless. Payment clause, which includes such aspects as amount, time, place, currencies, modes, and instruments of payment, is very important in an international sales contract. Letter of credit (L/C), collection, and remittance are three major modes of payment. But usually bills of exchange will be used in these modes of payment. A bill of exchange is a written order to a bank or a customer to pay someone on demand or at a fixed time in the future a certain sum of money. It is also called a draft or simply a bill.

Letter of Credit

Letter of credit (L/C) is the most widely used mode of payment by committing the bank to honor drafts and/or documents presented by the exporter who performs in strict accordance with the L/C stipulations. It is a reliable and safe method of payment facilitating trade with unknown buyers and giving protection to both sellers and buyers. A letter of credit is a written promise of a bank that acts at the request and on the instruction of the applicant and undertakes to pay the beneficiary the amount specified in the credit, provided that the terms and conditions of the credit are observed by the beneficiary. The disadvantage of this method of payment is the cost, which is to be borne on the importer for opening an L/C; the cost is usually higher than other means of payment, and it takes a longer time.

Collection

Collection is a paying arrangement under which the exporter, as drawer of a bill of exchange, hands the bill of exchange to his bank, who in turn forwards it to the buyer through a collection bank in the buyer's country. There are two types of collection: clean collection and documentary collection.

A collection is a "clean" one if the seller only draws a bill of exchange on the buyer without handing over any shipping documents to him; if it is one under which shipping documents accompany the bill of exchange, the collection is known as "documentary collection". Documentary collection falls into two major categories: document against payment (D/P) and document against acceptance (D/A).

Remittance

As the simplest method of payment in international trade, remittance means that the payer (usually the buyer) remits a certain sum of money in accordance with the parties' agreement to the payee (usually the seller) through a bank. This method of payment is often used for down payment, payment of commission and for samples, settlement of claim, or as performance bond, etc. Based on the means of transferring funds, a remittance usually falls into the following three types: mail transfer (M/T), telegraphic transfer (T/T), and demand draft (D/D).

Exercises

I. **Read the passage and choose the best answer to each question.**

1. Which of the following is the most widely used mode of payment?

A. Letter of credit.   B. Collection.

C. Mail transfer.   D. Telegraphic transfer.

2. What is the disadvantage of L/C?

    A. High speed.

    B. Safety.

    C. High cost.

    D. Usually used for payment of commission.

3. According to the passage, which of the following is used in the three major modes of payment?

    A. Mail.   B. Bill of exchange.

    C. Insurance document.   D. Packing document.

4. For the letter of credit, which characteristic is NOT involved?

    A. L/C is reliable and safe.

    B. L/C gives protection to both sellers and buyers.

    C. The L/C is given at the request of the buyer.

    D. The applicant has to observe the terms and conditions specified in the L/C.

5. For remittance, it is often used for small sum of money like _____.

    A. down payment

    B. payment of commission

    C. settlement of claim

    D. all of the above

II. Decide whether the statements are true (T) or false (F) according to the passage.

1. Payment is a complex part in the course of international trade. (　)

2. A bill of exchange is a written request to a bank or a customer to pay someone on demand or at a fixed time in the future a certain sum of money. (　)

3. L/C is a written promise of the bank. (　)

4. Under collection, the exporter draws a bill of exchange, hands it to his bank and then sends it to the buyer by himself. (　)

5. Remittance is the simplest method of payment in international trade. (　)

Section 2 Circulation Process of Documentary L/C

In international trade, the buyer and the seller may not trust each other. The buyer is worried that the seller will not deliver the goods according to the contract after payment in advance. The seller is also concerned that the buyer will not pay for the goods after delivery or presentation of shipping documents.

A letter of credit is a written undertaking, given at the request of the buyer, by the buyer's bank (the issuing bank) to pay a seller (the beneficiary), usually through an advising or negotiating bank in the beneficiary's country, provided the terms and conditions of the credit are complied with the contract, and documents called for by the credit are presented within the time limit specified.

The letter of credit ensures secured transaction, and it brings great convenience for both the buyer and the seller. With the guarantee of the bank, even in the face of distant and unfamiliar customers, there is no need to worry about the credit of the other party. Therefore, L/C is the most reliable mode of payment.

Here is the circulation process of a documentary L/C:

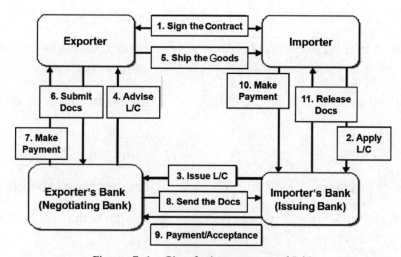

Figure 7–1   Circulation process of L/C

Exercises

I. Decide whether the statements are true (T) or false (F) according to the passage.

1. It is difficult for the buyer and the seller to trust each other in international trade. (   )

2. The seller is worried that the buyer will not pay for the goods after delivery of the goods. (   )

3. A letter of credit is a written undertaking, given at the request of the seller. (   )

4. The bank will not pay the seller if he does not observe the terms and conditions of the credit. (   )

5. With the guarantee of the bank, the seller and the buyer are still concerned about the credit of each other because of the distance in international trade. (   )

II. Match the words and phrases in the left column with their translations in the middle column and definitions in the right column.

1. applicant   A. 支付   a. the bank that opens L/C

2. beneficiary   B. 开证行   b. to pay for the seller or beneficiary

3. payment in advance   C. 受益人   c. a particular way of paying for something

4. negotiating bank   D. 支付方式   d. the party that receives the L/C

5. issuing bank   E. 交单   e. to give the documents to someone

6. mode of payment   F. 申请人   f. payment made before delivery

7. release documents   G. 议付行   g. the party that applies for issuing L/C

8. make payment   H. 预付款   h. the bank that pays the beneficiary

Part ② Case Study

In this part, you are supposed to read four letters on negotiating the terms of payment.

Letter 1: Negotiating terms of payment

Situation: *Guangzhou Tiande International Trade Co. Ltd. is an export company mainly engaged in automobile parts. At present, it has reached a preliminary transaction with Murklins Company of the United States. However, they have not reached a consensus on the payment method, so Tiande Co. writes a letter to Murklins Company, asking to make payment by letter of credit.*

Dear Carson,

We are very pleased to have **concluded a transaction** of 50,000 pieces of GTC automobile parts, and we have confirmed all the terms except for the terms of payment.

We are writing to inform you that our **usual practice** of payment is made by confirmed, irrevocable L/C in favor of our company, **payable by sight draft**. The L/C shall arrive one month ahead of shipment. It is valid for 15 days after the **stipulated** date of shipment, to be **negotiated** in China.

You are kindly requested to open the L/C at your earliest convenience, for the earlier we receive your L/C, the sooner we can arrange the shipment.

Look forward to your early reply.

Yours faithfully,

Fancie Yuan

Letter 2: Accepting terms of payment

Situation: *Murklins Company of the United States writes a letter in reply to Guangzhou Tiande International Trade Co. Ltd., accepting payment by letter of credit.*

Dear Fancie,

Thank you very much for your efforts in fulfilling the order. As this is our first order in Guangzhou, in order to show our great sincerity, we are willing to accept payment by L/C, even though the total amount is small and it's expensive to open L/C and **tie up** the capital of a small company like us.

We have **submitted to** Bank of America, Chicago Branch, an application for the issuing of a documentary letter of credit in your favor. Please prepare the following documents to **facilitate transaction**: ocean bill of lading in duplicate, commercial invoice in triplicate, packing list in triplicate, certificate of origin in duplicate.

We'll inform you once the L/C is opened.

Best regards,

Carson

Letter 3: Urging to open the L/C

Situation: *UBA Company of India and Dongli Trading Co. Ltd. in Guangzhou, China have entered into a transaction. Based on the sales contract signed by both parties, UBA shall open the letter of credit by June 28th. But due to certain reasons, the L/C has not been received. So the salesman Jaxton from Dongli is writing a letter to urge the establishment of L/C.*

Dear Mr. Sameer,

We inform you that the goods under S/C No. 20220615 have been ready for shipment for quite some time. They should be shipped during July as per the stipulation of our S/C.

We sent you an email two weeks ago requiring you to establish the covering L/C. However, much to our disappointment, we have not received any reply up to this moment. The time of shipment is approaching and we have to point out that we shall not be in a position to make the shipment **in due course** unless your L/C reaches us before July 10th. Therefore, please **expediate** the establishment of relevant L/C, so that we may execute the order smoothly.

In addition, you should ensure that the contents of L/C should be strictly **in conformity with** those of our contract.

Yours faithfully,

Jaxton

Letter 4: Asking for amendment of the L/C

Situation: *After receiving the L/C issued by Canadian Green Company, Guangzhou Zhongyuan Import and Export Co. Ltd. examined the documents carefully and found that there were three discrepancies compared with the contract, so the salesman of Zhongyuan is writing a letter to ask Green Company to amend the discrepancies in the L/C.*

Dear Christopher,

We are in receipt of your L/C No. 8421 established against S/C No. 20220615, but we regret to say that we have found some **discrepancies** between the L/C and the S/C after examining them carefully. Hereby the discrepancies are listed as follows for your attention.

1. Please delete the word "about" before the quantity in your L/C.

2. The amount in your L/C appears insufficient. Please increase the amount by $850.

3. As there is no direct steamer from Guangzhou to your port during July, it is imperative for you to delete the clause "by direct steamer" and insert the wording "partial shipment and transshipment are allowed".

We would like you to make the necessary **amendments** immediately.

As you know, we will be unable to make shipment unless the above discrepancies are corrected.

We look forward to receiving the amendment at an early date and thank you in advance.

Yours faithfully,

Dellica

Words and Expressions

1. conclude a transaction 达成交易

2. usual practice 惯例

3. payable by sight draft 凭即期汇票付款

4. stipulated *adj.* 规定的

5. negotiate *v.* 议付

6. tie up 占用

7. submit to... 向……提交

8. facilitate transaction 促进交易

9. in due course 在适当的时候

10. expediate *v.* 加速

11. in conformity with 与……一致

12. discrepancy *n.* 差异；不符合，不一致

13. amendment *n.* 修改

Exercises

Ⅰ. **Match the sentences with the key points of letters on negotiating terms of payment and finish the table below.**

1. The earlier we receive your L/C, the sooner we can arrange the shipment of goods.

2. We are glad that we have reached an agreement of 50,000 SNC automobile parts.

3. Please open an L/C without any delay to facilitate early shipment.

4. Our practice is to require the confirmed, irrevocable L/C payable by sight draft in favor of our company.

5. We are eager to know when you can open the relative L/C as the goods have been ready for shipment for quite a few days.

Key Points of Letters on Negotiating Terms of Payment	Sentences
State the mode of payment that you can accept	
Revert to the agreement you have reached	
Urge the buyer to establish the covering L/C with reasons	
Express your expectations	

II. **Match the sentences with the key points of letters on replying to negotiating terms of payment and finish the table below.**

1. We'll let you know once the L/C is opened.

2. As this is our first order in Guangzhou, in order to show our sincerity, we are willing to accept payment by L/C, even though the order amount is only US $50,000.

3. We have submitted to Bank of America, Los Angeles Branch, an application for the opening of a documentary letter of credit for $30,000.

4. Please prepare the following documents: ocean bill of lading in duplicate, commercial invoice in triplicate, packing list in triplicate, certificate of origin in duplicate.

5. With an eye to our future business, we'll agree to change the terms of payment from L/C at sight to T/T.

Key Points of Letters on Replying to Negotiating Terms of Payment	Sentences
Show agreement or disagreement on the payment with reasons	
Indicate the time when the L/C will be issued	

(Continued)

Key Points of Letters on Replying to Negotiating Terms of Payment	Sentences
Make other requirements	
Express your promise or expectations	

 III. Find the errors in the letter and improve it.

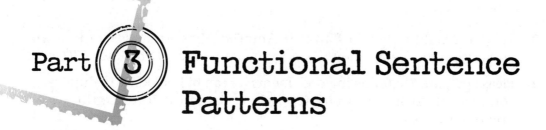

Sep. 5th, 2022

Dear Sirs,

We didn't get any information about the L/C. According to our contract, you should issue the L/C quickly. Please push this as soon as possible, or we must cancel this order and you should bear the cost.

Looking forward your earliest reply.

Yours sincerely,

Eric

Part ③ Functional Sentence Patterns

1. Negotiating Modes of Payment

(1) We propose to pay by bill of exchange at 30 days, documents against acceptance. Please confirm if this is acceptable to you.

(2) In order to show our great sincerity, we agree to accept payment by confirmed, irrevocable, and documentary L/C.

(3) It's expensive to open an L/C and tie up the capital of a small company like us, so it's better for us to adopt D/P or D/A.

(4) With an eye to our future business, we'll agree to change the terms of payment from L/C at sight to T/T.

(5) We regret having to inform you that although it is our desire to pave the way for a smooth development of business between us, we cannot accept payment by L/C.

2. Urging the Establishment of L/C

(1) Please do your utmost to expedite the covering L/C so that we may execute the order on time.

(2) We should ask you to rush the establishment of the L/C so that we may effect shipment by the direct steamer this month.

(3) As stipulated in the S/C No. 3217, you should open the relevant L/C before September 10th.

(4) As the goods ordered are ready for shipment, please hasten our L/C, and we will ship the order upon receipt of it.

(5) In order to execute your order No. 308, please urgently open an irrevocable L/C in our favor, available until December 30th. As the shipping time is near, we ask you to instruct your bankers to open it so that we can receive it within this week.

3. Notifying the Establishment of L/C

(1) As you have confirmed the order, we have arranged with Bank of China to open an L/C in your favor for the amount in accordance with the trade terms stipulated.

(2) We have made email instructions to our Los Angeles Branch to establish an L/C in favor of the Pacific Trading Co. Ltd., Los Angeles for the amount of $50,000.

(3) According to your request for opening an L/C, we are pleased to inform you that we have airmailed today through Bank of China an irrevocable L/C for $300,000 in favor of the New York Trading Co. Ltd. on the following terms and conditions.

(4) We hasten to inform you that we have today been informed by Bank of China of the establishment of an L/C in your favor for the amount of $800,000 available on or before July 30th.

(5) We wish to draw your attention to the fact that the relevant L/C will reach you tomorrow.

4. **Amending the L/C**

(1) Much to our regret, there are some discrepancies between our contract and the L/C.

(2) Please amend "transshipment is allowed" to read "transshipment is prohibited".

(3) The word "about" should be put before the quantity and amount in the L/C.

(4) Please amend L/C No. AO153 to read "This L/C will expire on July 12, 2022".

(5) We look forward to receiving the relevant amendment at an early date for the relative L/C.

Part ④ Situational Dialogs

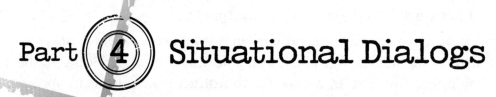

Dialog 1: *Lin is from Guangdong Silin International Trading Co. Ltd., an export company mainly engaged in toys. At present, Lin intends to conclude the transaction with Hany, the salesperson from an import company in the U.S.A. Now, they are negotiating terms of payment.*

Hany: We are very glad to have reached an agreement with you on 60,000 pieces of toys. All the terms and conditions have been confirmed except the terms of payment.

Lin: Well, it is our usual practice to ask for payment by confirmed, irrevocable letter of credit.

Hany: It's expensive to open an L/C and tie up the capital of a small company like us. So, it's better for us to adopt D/P or D/A.

Lin: We are sorry to advise you that the said terms of payment do not correspond to our customary business practice.

Hany: We regret that although it is our desire to pave the way for a smooth development of business between us, we cannot accept payment by L/C.

Lin: Emm, as a special accommodation, how about making payment of 50% by T/T in advance and the balance by L/C at sight? However, for future transactions, we hope that L/C will be accepted for the full invoice value.

Hany: Thanks a lot. The advance payment will be transferred to your bank account within the stipulated date.

Lin: That will be fine. Thanks for your cooperation.

Dialog 2: *One month later, Lin did not receive the L/C. Hence, she called Hany to urge him to open the L/C.*

Hany: Good morning. Can I help you?

Lin: Hello, this is Lin speaking, from Guangdong Silin International Trading Co. Ltd. We have concluded a transaction one month ago.

Hany: Oh, I see. It is about 60,000 pieces of toys.

Lin: Yes, you are right. In accordance with the contract, you are kindly requested to open the L/C within 20 days after signing the contract. However, up to this moment, we have not received your L/C yet.

Hany: I'm sorry to hear that. There are possibilities of something wrong with the accounting department.

Lin: Please do your best to expedite the covering L/C, so that we may execute the order smoothly. You know, the goods have been ready for shipment for quite a few days.

Hany: OK, sorry again. We will open the relative L/C as soon as possible.

Lin: Very good. Thank you for your cooperation. We sincerely hope that the L/C will reach us soon, or we shall be unable to effect shipment within the stipulated time limit.

Hany: Please be assured that the L/C will be opened immediately.

Lin: Great! Hope everything goes well.

Work in pairs and make a business dialog with your partner on payment according to the information given in the cue cards.

Cue Card A

You are Mr./Ms. Huang, a salesperson in an import company. You need to:

- ask for the mode of payment;
- ask whether D/A or D/P is acceptable;
- suggest for half D/P and half L/C with reasons.

Cue Card B

You are Mr./Ms. Black, a salesperson in an export company. You need to:

- suggest 100% value, confirmed, and irrevocable letter of credit;
- disagree with reasons;
- disagree but promise to talk about it with the manager.

Part ⑤ Skill Training

I. Match the words and phrases in the left column with their translations in the right column.

1.	usual practice	A. 与……相一致
2.	in duplicate	B. 议付
3.	in conformity with	C. 修改
4.	negotiate	D. 确认
5.	amendment	E. 惯例

6. confirm   F. 商业发票

7. for one's account   G. 一式两份

8. commercial invoice   H. 履行订单

9. fulfill the order   I. 凭汇票付款

10. payable by draft   J. 由某人支付

II. **Fill in the blanks with appropriate words or phrases given in the box.**

approaching	under	reaches	received
ready	stipulated	unless	in conformity with

June 25th, 2022

Dear Sirs,

We inform you that the goods **1.** _____ S/C No. 2576 have been **2.** _____ for shipment for quite some time. They should be shipped during October as **3.** _____ in S/C. However, much to our disappointment, we have not **4.** _____ any reply up to the moment.

The time of shipment is **5.** _____ and we have to point out that we shall not be in a position to make the shipment in due course **6.** _____ your L/C **7.** _____ us before the end of this month.

In addition, you should ensure that the contents of L/C should be strictly **8.** _____ those of our contract.

Looking forward to your reply.

Yours faithfully,

Alex

III. **Choose the best answer to complete each of the following sentences.**

1. _____ you fulfill the terms of the L/C, we will accept the drafts drawn under this credit.

A. Provided   B. To provide

C. Supplied   D. Furnished

2. It needs _____ that the L/C should reach us 30 days before the month of shipment.

    A. being mentioned   B. to be mentioned

    C. mentioned   D. mention

3. As stipulated in the contract, the bank _____ open an L/C before the end of September 2022.

    A. will   B. ought

    C. need   D. shall

4. We advised our bank to _____ L/C No. 12345 to read "partial shipments to be permitted".

    A. change   B. amend

    C. alter   D. add

5. The consignment will be dispatched as soon as possible _____ to reach the final destination by mid-August.

    A. as   B. so

    C. so as   D. so that

6. Please note that the goods you ordered can be certainly promised for immediate shipment _____ receipt of your L/C.

    A. upon   B. with

    C. in   D. without

7. As the goods are ready for shipment, we _____ your L/C to be opened immediately.

    A. hope   B. anticipate

    C. await   D. expect

8. Payment of the purchase is to be made _____ confirmed, irrevocable L/C.

    A. by   B. of

    C. for   D. from

9. Your full cooperation in this respect will be highly _____.

    A. thanked   B. appreciating

    C. thanking   D. appreciated

10. Should your L/C _____ us at the beginning of June, we shall be able to ship your order.

A. arrive   B. reach

C. come   D. get

IV. **Translate the following sentences into English or Chinese respectively.**

1. 最好用不可撤销可转让信用证。

2. 我们不明白为什么你方的信用证还没有到达我方。

3. 我们已收到你方信用证，但遗憾的是，我们仔细检查后发现有不符之处。

4. 我们期待早日收到修正函，并预先表示感谢。

5. 很抱歉，由于供应商的延误，我们无法在本月底前备好货物。

6. Please open an L/C without any delay to facilitate early shipment.

7. In order to show our great sincerity, we agree to accept payment by confirmed, irrevocable, and documentary L/C.

8. We are sorry to inform you that the listed terms of payment do not correspond to our customary business practice.

9. We enclose the transaction voucher for your reference.

10. Please do your best to expedite the covering L/C, so that we may execute the order smoothly.

V. **Write a business letter according to the following situation.**

You are an exporter of household appliances in Guangzhou, China. After entering into a transaction of hair dryers with Jackson Import Company of the United States for payment by L/C, you have not received the L/C in time. Therefore, you are going to urge the importer to open the L/C.

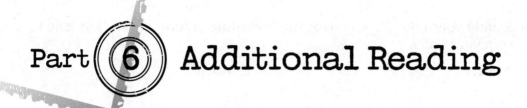

Part 6 Additional Reading

Documentary Credit

Issuing Bank:	METTTABANK LTD., FINLAND
Form of DOC. Credit:	IRREVOCABLE
Credit Number:	LRT2204457
Date of Issue:	220428
Expiry:	DATE 220616 PLACE CHINA
Applicant:	F. T. C. CO.
	AKEKSANTERINK AUTO
	P. O. BOX 9, FINLAND
Beneficiary:	GREAT WALL TRADING CO., LTD.
	RM201, HUASHENG BUILDING, NINGBO, P. R. OF CHINA
Amount:	USD 36,408.00 (SAY U.S. DOLLARS THIRTY SIX THOUSAND FOUR HUNDRED AND EIGHT ONLY)
Available with/by:	ANY BANK IN ADVISING COUNTRY BY NEGOTIATION
Draft at…:	DRAFTS AT 30 DAYS SIGHT FOR FULL INVOICE VALUE
Partial Shipment:	NOT ALLOWED
Transshipment:	ALLOWED
Loading in Charge:	NINGBO
For Transport to:	HELSINKI
Shipment Period:	AT THE LATEST MAY 30, 2022
Descrip. of Goods:	960 PCS OF HALOGEN FITTING W 500, USD 6.80 PER PC AS PER SALES CONTRACT GW2022 DATED APRIL 4, 2022 CIF HESINKI
Documents Required:	* COMMERCIAL INVOICE 1 SIGNED ORIGINAL AND 5 COPIES
	* PACKING LIST IN 2 COPIES

* FULL SET OF CLEAN ON BOARD MARINE BILL OF LADING, MADE OUT TO ORDER, MARKED "FREIGHT PREPAID" AND NOTIFY APPLICANT (AS INDICATE ABOVE)

* GSP CERTIFICATE OF ORIGIN FORM A, CERTIFY GOODS OF ORIGIN IN CHINA, ISSUED BY COMPETENT AUTHORITIES

* INSURANCE POLICY / CERTIFICATE COVERING ALL RISKES AND WAR RISK OF PICC. INCLUDING WAREHOUSE TO WAREHOUSE CLAUSE UP TO FINAL DESTINATION AT HELSINKI, FOR AT LEAST 120 PCT OF CIF VALUE

* SHIPPING ADVICES MUST BE SENT TO APPLICANT WITHIN 2 DAYS AFTER SHIPMENT ADVISING NUMBER OF PACKAGES, GROSS WEIGHT AND NET WEIGHT, VESSEL NAME, BILL OF LADING NO. AND DATE, CONTRACT NO., VALUE

Presentation Period: 15 DAYS AFTER ISSUANCE DATE OF SHIPPING DOCUMENT

Confirmation: WITHOUT

Instructions: THE NEGOTIATION BANK MUST FORWARD THE DRAFTS AND DOCUMENTS BY REGISTERED AIRMAIL DIRECT TO US IN TWO CONSECUTIVE LOTS. UPON RECEIPT OF THE DRAFTS AND DOCUMENTS IN ORDER, WE WILL REMIT THE PROCEEDS AS INSTRUCTED BY THE NEGOTIATION BANK

Chapter 8

Packing

Learning Objectives

By completing this unit, students will learn:

- types of packing and packing marks in international trade;
- how to analyze case letters on packing;
- useful expressions and sentence patterns related to packing;
- how to negotiate on packing.

Lead-in

Work in groups, discuss the following questions and then share your answers with the whole class.

1. What are the functions of packing?

2. Can you list some items usually appearing on the package?

3. In international trade, what aspects of packing should be considered?

4. What constituents should be included in a letter on packing requirements?

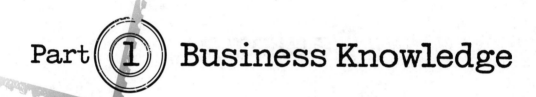

Part ① Business Knowledge

Section 1 What Is Packing?

In international trade, most goods need packing. Packing is one of the essential components of commodity production. Packing can protect the commodity and keep it good in quality and intact in quantity during the distribution process. At the same time, it can increase the market value of the goods. It protects the goods from damage, makes it easy to be identified, enables manufacturers, sellers, and customers to move goods from place to place freely, and helps the sellers to push the sales of goods.

The kinds of cargoes are various in international trade, but from the view point of whether they need packing, they fall into three kinds.

Nude cargoes or nude packed commodities refer to those kinds of cargoes whose qualities are more stable and can be shipped without any packages or in simple bundles. They are not easy to be influenced by outside circumstances and they become single pieces of their own. They are difficult to be packed or do not need any packing, such as steel products, lead ingot, timber, rubber, automobile, etc.

The second type of goods is called bulk cargoes, which refer to the goods whose qualities are also so stable that they don't need to be packed, or it's very difficult or even impossible to have them packed, for instance, iron ore, grain, coal, etc. Bulk shipment is usually applicable for large quantity of commodities that are to be shipped by means of transport with special purposed shipping equipment. Bulk shipment has the advantages of space saving, quick handling, and lower freight.

Most of commodities in international trade need certain degree of packing during the shipping, storing, and sales process. Packed cargoes refer to those that need shipping packing, marketing packing, or both. Shipping packing is also called big packing or outer packing, and it helps transportation. Cargoes need to be packed in different ways, such as in wooden cases（木箱）, crates（板条箱）, cartons（纸箱）, bales（包）, bundles（捆）, barrels（桶）, iron drums（铁桶）, gunny bags（麻袋）, kraft paper bags（牛皮纸）, pallets（托盘）, and many others. Marketing packing is also called small, sales or inner packing. The function of marketing packing is to protect the goods as well as to beautify and introduce them to customers.

Exercises

I. **Read the passage and choose the best answer to each question.**

1. Which of the following is NOT the function of packing?

A. To protect the goods from damage.

B. To help the sellers push sales.

C. To move goods from place to place more easily and more freely.

D. To establish and maintain business relations.

2. Which of the following is NOT nude cargo?

A. Steel products.   B. Timber.

C. Coal.   D. Rubber.

3. The following are reasons why it is not necessary to pack bulk cargos EXCEPT that _____.

A. their qualities are stable

B. it's very difficult or even impossible to have them packed

C. they are easy to be influenced by outside circumstances

D. they needn't be packed

4. Shipping packing or outer packing is used for_____.

    A. helping transportation   B. beautification of goods

    C. pushing sales   D. introducing goods

5. Which of the following statements is NOT true according to the passage?

    A. Packing is important in international trade.

    B. It is not necessary to negotiate on the packing requirements when the sales contract or sales confirmation is signed.

    C. It is not necessary to pack steel products, lead ingot, timber, rubber, and automobiles.

    D. Bulk shipment is usually applicable for large quantity of commodities.

II. **Read the passage and answer the following questions.**

1. What are the three types of cargoes according to whether they need packing?

_____

2. What are the functions of packing?

_____

3. What is the difference between outer packing and inner packing?

_____

Section 2 Packing Marks

According to the uses, packing marks can be divided into the following four categories—shipping marks, indicative marks, warning marks, and supplementary (or additional) marks.

Shipping marks are marks of simple designs, some letters, numbers, and simple words on packages, often stenciled, that serve as identification of the consignment to which they belong. It is one of the most important elements that are agreed on by the exporter and the importer in a sales contract. The shipping mark consists of the consignor's or the consignee's code name, number of the contract of the L/C, the port of destination, and the number of the packed goods.

The second is indicative marks. We usually make use of the simple, noticeable designs, remarkable diagrams, and simple words on the packages to remind the relative workers of the items for attention when they load, unload, carry, and store the goods, such as "HANDLE WITH CARE" and "THIS SIDE UP", printed in black color generally.

The warning marks are also called dangerous cargo marks or shipping marks for dangerous commodities, which are brushed/printed clearly and definitely on the outer packing of the inflammable, explosive, poisonous, corrosive or radioactive goods, so as to give warnings to the workers/dockers/crew.

Supplementary marks are any official marks required by authorities. Some countries require the country of origin to be marked on every package, and weight and dimensions may also be required.

Packing terms in the contract are extremely important for the exporter. They are often written in this way: "Goods must be packed in…" Sometimes the buyer may ask the exporter to pack the goods in his design. If his requirements can be met by the exporter, the exporter can accept the terms. Otherwise, try to persuade the buyer to adopt the exporter's own or traditional packing instead. Any changes regarding packing stipulated in the contract should be mutually discussed and determined before shipment.

Exercises

I. Decide whether the statements are true (T) or false (F) according to the passage.

1. Shipping marks often contain elaborate designs to serve as identification of the consignment. (   )

2. "NO HOOK" and "KEEP DRY" are shipping marks. (   )

3. "INFLAMMABLE" and "EXPLOSIVE" are indicative marks. (   )

4. "MADE IN CHINA" and "NEW YORK" are warning marks. (   )

5. Packing terms in the contract are extremely important for the exporter. (   )

II. Match the phrases in the left column with their translations in the right column.

1. packing mark   A. 警示性标志

2. long distance ocean transportation
3. shipping mark
4. indicative mark
5. warning mark
6. handle with care

B. 指示性标志

C. 小心轻放

D. 包装标志

E. 运输标志

F. 长途海运

Part ② Case Study

In this part, you are supposed to read four letters on making packing requirements and the replies.

Letter 1: Packing requirements

Situation: *Lin Xin has received an email from Mr. Kouki, the sales manager of Supreme Food Supply Co. Ltd. based in Kyoto, Japan. Mr. Kouki's company has signed a contract to import tea from Lin Xin's company in Guangzhou, but details regarding packing are not specific. His email elaborates on the requirements of packing.*

Dear Mr. Lin,

We acknowledge receipt of your letter dated July 4th enclosing the S/C No. 1695 in duplicate. After **going through** the contract, we find that the **packing clause** in it is not clear enough.

In order to avoid possible trouble, we would like to make clear beforehand our packing requirements as follows:

The tea under the **captioned contract** should be packed in internationally used tea boxes, 24 boxes to a carton, 280 cartons to a pallet, 20 pallets to an **FCL** container. On the outer packing, please mark our initials "SFS" in a diamond, under which the port of destination and our order number should be **stenciled**. In addition, indicative marks "KEEP DRY" and "USE NO HOOKS" should also be noted.

In addition, the packing must be **seaworthy** and strong enough to stand rough handling, and prevent skillful **pilferage**. Would you please tell us whether these requirements could be met? We look forward to receiving your favorable reply.

Thank you in advance.

Yours faithfully,

Kage Kouki

Letter 2: Reply to packing requirements

Situation: *Zhang Guoming, the sales manager of Guangzhou Hardware Incorporation is writing an email in reply to Mr. Harding's email enquiring about the export packing of their staplers. He stresses the advantages of his company's packing.*

Dear Mr. Harding,

In reply to your email of July 5th enquiring about the packing of our staplers covered by order No. 173, we wish to state as follows:

- Our staplers for export are first put in a poly bag, and then packed in boxes of one dozen each, 120 boxes to a carton.

- The **dimensions** are 20 cm high, 30 cm wide and 50 cm long with a **volume** of about 0.028 cubic meters per carton.

- The **gross weight** is 24.5 kg, and the **net weight** is 23.5 kg per carton.

- In addition to the gross, net, and **tare weight**, the shipping marks outside the carton also include the words: "MADE IN CHINA".

In order to avoid scratches and knocks against each other, we wrap and pad all **polished** parts of the stapler with foam plastics in thick and exquisite paper boxes lined with waterproof paper. Meanwhile, cartons have been proved light, compact, and easy for handling during transportation, which have gained our customers' satisfaction in previous transactions. Therefore, you can rest assured that the packing mentioned above will guarantee our products' perfect condition in transit and on arrival.

Should you have any special preference **in this respect**, please let us know and we will meet you to the best of our ability.

Sincerely yours,

Zhang Guoming

Letter 3: Complaint about improper packing

Situation: *David Colton, a sales manager in Saint Louis Machinery Co. Ltd., is writing a letter complaining about the broken loudspeakers due to improper packing to Pierson Wu, trading coordinator of Guangzhou Better Electric Appliance Company. David hopes to improve packing for future orders to avoid damage during transit.*

Dear Pierson,

Our latest order of loudspeakers has been received with thanks.

Reverting to the 5 lots of loudspeakers under contract No. 623 which arrived here by S/S "Twilight" on July 20th, we regret to inform you that owing to improper packing, **in the same hold**, several packages arrived in such a bad condition that we were compelled to dispose of them at greatly reduced prices.

Though such unfortunate things happened before and we have reminded you of the necessity to strengthen straps on the cartons, or any other improvement **to that effect**, the present situation reveals that our suggestions were ignored, as the poor packing was evident in each broken package.

Consequently, we would like to have you promise to take effective measures to enhance packing before we can **renew the order**.

Yours faithfully,

David Colton

Letter 4: Replying to improper packing

Situation: *Pierson Wu is writing an email in response to an email sent by David Colton, who complains about the mixed condition of the consignment caused by insufficient packing. He explains why the damages occurred and promises to take effective measures to improve packing for future orders.*

Dear David,

I am sorry to receive your email about the mixed and broken packages under contract No. 623. Fortunately, only 23 pieces in the 10 cartons were confirmed damaged and must be **disposed**.

We immediately **dispatched** qualified **surveyors** to enquire into the matter and their findings show that this was due to rough handling in transit or unloading. The goods under the above contract were in perfect condition when they were shipped, and individual packages were clearly marked with "HANDLE WITH CARE", "KEEP DRY", and other necessary indicative marks. B/L shows our procedures were complete and appropriate.

You may be aware that our loudspeakers have been sold in a number of markets abroad for quite a long time, and all our customers have been satisfied with our packing. Each shipment is strictly inspected by our shipping department before loading and each package is subject to careful examination. Therefore, we consider it a matter for you to **take up with** the shipping company or the insurance company who has covered the said **consignment**. However, to avoid prospective loss, we decide to modify our packing by **reinforcing** the cartons **with** double straps though the damage was not our fault.

As your long-term partner, we value your friendship and trust, and assure you of our commitment to execute the order effectively. I am sure no such thing will happen again in future deliveries.

We appreciate your cooperation.

Yours faithfully,

Pierson Wu

Words and Expressions

1. go through 通读，查阅

2. packing clause 包装条款

3. captioned contract 标题所指的合同

4. FCL=full container load 整箱

5. stencil *v.* 刷唛

6. seaworthy *adj.*（船）经得起风浪的，适宜航海的

7. pilferage *n.* 偷窃

8. dimension *n.* 维度；尺寸

9. volume *n.* 体积，容积，容量

10. gross weight 毛重

11. net weight 净重

12. tare weight 皮重

13. polished *adj.* 抛光的，磨光的

14. in this respect 在这一方面

15. in the same hold 在同一货舱内

16. to that effect 大意是那样的，诸如此类的

17. renew the order 续订单

18. dispose *v.* 处置

19. dispatch *v.* 派遣

20. surveyor *n.* 检验员

21. take up with... 与……交涉

22. consignment *n.* 发送的货物

23. reinforce...with... 用……加固

Exercises

I. Match the sentences with the key points of letters on enquiring about packing and finish the table below.

1. In order to avoid any possible trouble, we would like to make the packing requirements as follows.

2. Because of the limited container space, the overall measurements of each case must not exceed 1.5 m × 1 m × 1 m.

3. The products should be packed in strong cartons, each containing 8 bags.

4. The goods will be packed in iron drums of 25 kgs net each, 6 drums to a crate.

5. In view of precaution, please mark "FRAGILE" and "HANDLE WITH CARE" on the outer packing.

6. The machines must be well protected against dampness, moisture, rust, and shock.

7. Every 100 dozen should be packed in a wooden case marked "ABC" and numbered from No. 1 upward.

8. On the outer packing, please mark the country of origin, the port of discharge and the order number.

9. We are pleased to receive your letter of enquiry and wish to state as follows.

10. Our way of packing has been widely accepted by other clients, and we have received no complaints whatsoever up to now.

11. We look forward to receiving your early reply.

Key Points of Letters on Enquiring About Packing	Sentences
Show thanks or acknowledgement	
Give packing requirements in detail	
Explain reasons	
Show expectation	

II. **Find the errors in the letter and improve it.**

July 8th, 2022

Dear Sirs,

We are very pleasure to inform you that for your future orders, we shall pack our garments in cartons instead wooden cases, as pack in cartons have the following advantages:

- It will protect skillful pilferage as the traces of pilferage will be clearer in evidence.
- It is fairly fit long distance ocean transportation.
- Our cartons are well protected against moisture by plastic line.
- Cartons are comparative light and compact, so they are more convenient to handle.

We hope you will accept our carton pack and assure you of our sincere cooperation.

Yours sincerely,

Jeff

Part ③ Functional Sentence Patterns

1. Giving Packing Instructions

(1) In order to avoid any possible trouble, we would like to make the packing requirements as follows.

(2) The machines must be well protected against dampness, moisture, rust, and shock.

(3) The packing must be strong enough to withstand rough handling in transit.

(4) We have especially reinforced our packing in order to minimize the extent of any damage to the goods.

(5) The products should be packed in strong cartons, each containing 8 bags.

(6) The products are customarily packed in boxes of 20 pieces each, 80 boxes to a carton, 650 cartons to a 20 feet container.

2. Negotiating Ways of Packing

(1) This kind of packing does not cost more, and it can effectively protect the goods from being damaged by rough handling.

(2) Packing in cartons has become popular in international shipment and insurance companies are ready to accept it for WPA and TPND.

(3) Our way of packing has been widely accepted by other clients, and we have received no complaints whatsoever up to now.

(4) In view of precaution, please mark "FLEXIBLE" and "FRAGILE" on each package.

(5) All the bags are beautifully designed to come in line with the local market preference at your end.

(6) Cartons are comparatively light and compact, more convenient to handle in the course of loading and unloading, and quite fit for ocean transportation.

3. Complaining About Improper Packing

(1) We regret to inform you that the 10 cartons of dishware you shipped to us in June were badly damaged.

(2) Our investigation shows that damage was caused by improper packing. Therefore, we have to refer this matter to you.

(3) Owing to faulty packing, several of them arrived in such a bad condition that we were compelled to dispose of them at greatly reduced prices.

(4) We accept that the damage was not your fault but feel that you must modify your packing requirements to avoid future losses.

(5) The suppliers should be held responsible for short weight resulting from improper packing.

(6) Please take effective measures to improve your packing before we could make this new order with you.

Part ④ Situational Dialogs

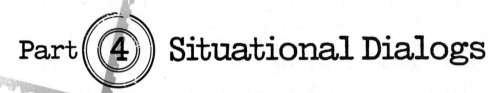

Dialog 1: *After the problem regarding the terms of payment had been settled, Mr. White, a businessman from Austria, prompted the subject of packing with Miss Yang, the marketing manager from North Fashion Import and Export Company.*

White: Miss Yang, our clients have great interest in your men's shirt.

Yang: I'm glad to hear that.

White: They paid special attention to the cardboard boxes.

Yang: These boxes do add to the value of the gift, don't you think so?

White: Yes, it would be better to make the logo on the shirts a little smaller though.

Yang: Right, I'll take care of that for you. What do you think of the packing for shirts?

White: I think you must have your own way of packing garments.

Yang: Yes, we use a polythene wrapper for each shirt, quite suitable for window display.

White: Good, the inner packing should be tasteful and eye-catching. Attractive packing promotes the sales. With keen competition, the merchandise must not only be of good value, but also look attractive. What about the outer packing?

Yang: We'll pack them ten dozen to one carton, gross weight around twenty kilos a carton.

White: Cartons?

Yang: Yes, cartons made of paper board.

White: Why not use wooden cases?

Yang: The cartons are comparatively light and therefore easy to handle. They won't be stowed with other heavy cargoes. Shirts are not fragile goods, so they can stand lots of shaking. Besides, we'll reinforce the cartons with plastic straps.

White: But the goods will be transshipped. How could they be prevented from the damage of dampness and rain?

Yang: Don't worry about that. The cartons are to be lined with waterproof plastic sheets, absolutely safe.

White: Maybe so. I am quite concerned that in case our goods are damaged in transit, the insurance company will refuse compensation on the ground of improper packing or packing unsuitable for sea voyage.

Yang: But cartons are quite commonly used internationally in long-distance ocean transportation, Mr. White. There are never any complaints from our clients. And such packing has also been approved by our insurance company for WPA and TPND coverage.

White: If you could guarantee the compensation in case that the insurance company declines to honor a claim for such packing, we would be willing to accept cartons.

Yang: I am sorry, but we cannot take on the responsibility that is beyond our function and powers. We will make sure that the packing is seaworthy. Meanwhile, we cannot commit ourselves to be held responsible for every kind of loss.

White: I understand your position. Perhaps I am demanding too much.

Yang: We will use wooden cases, if you insist anyway. But the charges for that kind of packing will be considerably higher. And it also slows down the delivery.

White: Well, I will phone home immediately for the final confirmation on the matter.

Dialog 2: *Mr. White made a phone call with Miss Yang to complain about the damaged cartons which had just arrived in Perth.*

White: I think personal contact will help solve the problems between us.

Yang: I'm sorry for that.

White: Your last shipment discouraged us as mentioned in the previous correspondence. When the goods arrived at our port, some cartons were opened and unfortunately, we found some of the shirts were severely damaged.

Yang: I'm sorry to hear that. What's the comment of the independent surveyor?

White: They said the damage was caused by improper packing. So, I hope that this time you will improve your packing. To be more specific, add more padding inside the carton and use straps for outer reinforcement. Can you make it happen?

Yang: As I know, our packing has been tested for such transportation. There have never been such damages as you said. I wonder if it was due to rough handling.

White: I believe what the survey report said. Since we still have a lot of goods ready for shipment next week, we hope such things won't happen again.

Yang: I can assure you of that. I would like to send someone to inspect the damaged goods in order to improve our packaging.

White: It's worth your effort.

Yang: Yes, and we believe our future packing will be satisfactory to you.

White: As a proverb goes, "practice makes perfect".

Yang: That's right.

Exercise

Work in pairs and make a business dialog with your partner on packing according to the information given in the cue cards.

Cue Card A

> You are Mr./Ms. Hebe, sales manager of APL Export Company. You need to:
> - confirm the order with happiness;
> - ask for packing requirements;
> - agree and promise to pack the goods as required;
> - assure of strong packing.

Cue Card B

You are Mr./Ms. Hilly, the salesperson of Leading Import Company in the USA. You need to:

- greet and show your thanks;
- give packing instructions;
- emphasize the importance of strong packing;
- extend good expectation.

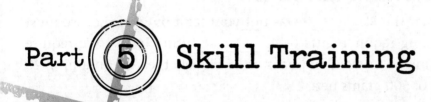

Part ⑤ Skill Training

I. Match the words and phrases in the left column with their translations in the right column.

1. seaworthy packing   A. 内衬 / 填充······

2. in transit   B. 调查

3. revert to   C. 适合海运的包装

4. water-proof   D. 刷唛

5. rough handling   E. 毛重

6. gross weight   F. 货舱

7. hold   G. 重提

8. stencil   H. 在运输途中

9. be lined/padded with···   I. 野蛮搬运

10. enquire into   J. 防水的

II. **Fill in the blanks with appropriate words given in the box.**

packages	in	received	inform	to
damage	met	packing	containing	avoid

July 5th, 2022

Dear Sirs,

Today we **1.** _____ your consignment of 40 cardboard cartons of safety pins. We regret to **2.** _____ you that 20 cartons were delivered damaged and the contents had spilled, leading to some losses.

We accept that the **3.** _____ was not your fault but feel that we must modify our packing requirements to **4.** _____ future losses. We require that future packing be in wooden boxes of 25 kilos net, each containing 40 cardboard packs of 500 grams net.

Please let us know whether these specifications can be **5.** _____ by you and whether they will lead to an increase in your price. Upon arrival of the goods at the port of destination, we found that nearly 20% of the **6.** _____ had been broken, obviously attributed to improper **7.** _____.

We suggest that the screws be packed **8.** _____ tins of 600 grams, 20 tins **9.** _____ one wooden case. Our screwdrivers are packed in cartons, each **10.** _____ 100 pieces. Please make sure that all the drums are strong enough and are up to international standard.

Sincerely yours,

Bill Lee

III. **Choose the best answer to complete each of the following sentences.**

1. The machines will be packed _____ specially designed crates.

A. by
B. of
C. at
D. in

2. The exporting sewing machines _____ in stout waterproof material, and _____ in pairs in lightweight crates.

A. being wrapped; are packed
B. are wrapped; packed

C. are wrapping; packing   D. are wrapped; being packed

3. In order to facilitate _____, it would be better to pack the goods in cases of 50 dozen each.

A. sales   B. to sell

C. it to sell   D. to selling

4. We have made it clear that the packing must be _____ to withstand rough handling.

A. enough strong   B. strong

C. strong enough   D. strongly enough

5. _____ there is no direct steamer to your port from Dalian, the goods have to be transshipped in other ports.

A. Being   B. Having

C. As   D. Because of

6. Please send us full instructions for the ten cases for London _____ contents, value, consignee, and who pays all the charges.

A. as to   B. to

C. regard to   D. concern

7. Due to a serious shortage of shipping space, we _____ deliver these machines_____ December.

A. can; except   B. can; in

C. cannot; unless   D. cannot; until

8. The goods _____ for shipment tomorrow.

A. are prepared   B. have prepared

C. will prepare   D. prepared

9. All powders are wrapped in plastic bags and packed in tins, _____ the lids are sealed with adhesive tape.

A. which   B. by which

C. of which   D. at which

10. Overall measurements of each case must not _____ 4 cm × 2 cm × 2 cm.

A. over   B. pass

C. exceed   D. appear

IV. Translate the following sentences into English or Chinese respectively.

1. 务请使用坚固的木箱装载。木箱必须钉牢，并且以金属绳带扣紧。

2. 请以 6 寸大小的字体标示警示标志、指示标志以及你们自己的标志，并同时注明毛重和净重。

3. 请以防水木箱包装，每 30 件装一箱。装运不得迟于 8 月 6 日。

4. 你们的包装必须具有适航性，并经得起运输途中的粗鲁搬运。

5. 我们会采取一切必要的预防措施，确保我们的产品完好无损地送到客户手中。

6. Pens are packed in boxes of a dozen each, 100 dozen to a carton.

7. In view of precaution, please mark "FRAGILE" and "HANDLE WITH CARE" on the outer packing.

8. Please pack the goods in a strong wooden case, and wrap and pad all polished parts of the machine to avoid scratches and knocks against the container.

9. We would like to make clear beforehand our packing requirements as follows: Packing should prevent skillful pilferage and withstand rough handling.

10. Please see to it that the wooden cases should be lined with waterproof material so that the goods can be protected against moisture.

V. Write a business letter according to the following situation.

You have concluded a transaction with your partner and now you are writing a letter to inform him that your usual practice for packing is in cardboard cartons instead of wooden cases. The following points of cardboard cartons should be covered in the letter:

- prevent skillful pilferage;
- fit for long distance ocean transportation;
- light and compact.

Part 6 Additional Reading

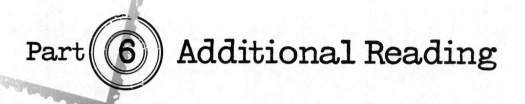

The Importance of Packing

Packing is of great importance in international trade. It may be appropriately said that packing is to goods as what clothing is to man. The ultimate purpose of packing is to keep the transported goods in perfect condition with nothing missing on arrival. Good packing must be able to stand the roughest transportation. Packing can be divided into transport packing (usually known as outer packing) and sales packing (usually known as inner packing).

Transport packing is done mainly to keep the goods safe and sound during transportation. It must not only be solid enough to prevent the packed goods from any damage, but also pilferage-proof, easy to store, convenient to load and unload. Sales packing is done mainly to push sales. It is now universally recognized as a decisive aid in selling household consumer goods. It can be realized in various forms and with different materials as long as it is nice to look, easy to handle, and helpful to the sales.

Still, there is another category of packing, called "neutral packing". This kind of packing carries no mark or the name of the origin country on the packed goods and no sign of the original trademark, with a view of satisfying the buyer's special requirements.

Chapter 9

Insurance

Learning Objectives

By completing this unit, students will learn:

- the importance of cargo insurance in international trade and basic types of cargo insurance in China;
- how to analyze case letters on insurance;
- useful expressions and sentence patterns related to insurance;
- how to negotiate on insurance.

Lead-in

Work in groups, discuss the following questions and then share your answers with the whole class.

1. Why is insurance so important in international trade?

2. What are the basic types of insurance in international trade?

3. Which party should cover insurance, the exporter or the importer?

4. What should be taken into consideration when you effect insurance?

5. What constituents should be included in a letter on insurance in international trade?

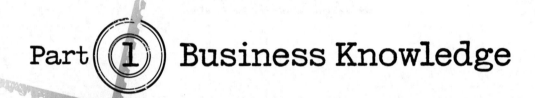

Part 1 Business Knowledge

Section 1 Covering Cargo Insurance

In international trade, the transportation of goods from the seller to the buyer is generally over a long distance by air, land, or sea, and has to go through the procedures of loading, unloading and storing. During this process, it is quite possible that the goods will encounter various kinds of perils and sometimes suffer losses. In order to protect the goods against possible losses in case of such perils, buyers or sellers usually apply to an insurance company for insurance covering the goods in transit.

When shipment is made to a foreign market, cargo insurance is strongly recommended. It is essential if the terms of sales require the seller to arrange insurance, for example a CIF contract. The cost of cargo insurance is nominal in most cases, amounting to less than 1% of the value of the shipment and the freight bill.

With the proper insurance policy, buyers or sellers can recover losses if their shipments are accidentally lost, stolen, damaged, or delayed, although the extent of recovery will depend on the type of insurance purchased.

Without insurance, they could have no recourse.

When covering insurance, buyers or sellers should consider several things, such as the amount of coverage (all risks or limited), time of year, route, and destination port (the North Atlantic during the winter months can be dangerous; some ports can have higher than usual rates of pilferage), the loss and damage record of competing carriers, and cargo stowage and packing.

Insurance should be looked at as part of the total rate and service package that the carrier offers, so don't look at insurance in isolation. Even though a carrier may not have any record of mistake, there is always an element of risk and buyers or sellers should protect themselves against this risk. Moreover, insurance coverage is part of a carrier's marketing strategy. It is more than likely that cost, coverage, and the number of loss and damage claims will vary from carrier to carrier, so buyers or sellers should make some comparisons.

Insurance can be arranged directly with a carrier, an insurer, an insurance broker or agent, or through a freight forwarder or customs broker. Whether the exporter purchases from a carrier or a third party, make sure that the insurance purchased covers the entire journey: That is from the time it leaves the seller's plant or warehouse until it is in the buyer's warehouse. In some instances, a carrier will provide coverage only when it is handling the shipment.

It should be noted that insurance for products such as dangerous goods and hazardous wastes are covered by separate insurance methods.

Exercises

I. **Read the passage and choose the best answer to each question.**

1. In most cases, the cost of cargo insurance is _____.

A. very high

B. very low

C. non-existent

D. fluctuating

2. In a CIF contract, _____.

A. it is the buyer who should arrange insurance

B. it is the seller who should arrange insurance

C. sometimes the cost of cargo insurance is more than 1% of the value of goods

D. the extent of recovery has nothing to do with the type of insurance purchased

3. According to the passage, _____ is one of the factors buyers or sellers should consider when they are arranging insurance.

A. the cost of insurance

B. the port of loading

C. the loss and damage record of competing carriers

D. reputation of the insurance company

4. Which of the following statements is true?

A. Insurance is isolated from the carrier's service package.

B. A carrier without any record of mistakes can guarantee buyers or sellers from risks.

C. When selecting insurance, the exporter can put trust in a particular carrier if they have kept a long-term business relationship.

D. Insurance coverage is part of a carrier's marketing strategy.

5. When arranging insurance from a carrier or a third party, buyers or sellers should make sure that the insurance purchased covers _____.

A. the journey from the port of loading to the buyer's warehouse

B. the journey from the seller's warehouse to the port of destination

C. the journey from the seller's warehouse to the buyer's warehouse

D. the journey from the port of loading to the port of destination

II. Decide whether the statements are true (T) or false (F) according to the passage.

1. In order to protect the goods against possible losses, the buyers or the sellers usually apply to an insurance company for insurance covering the goods in transit. (   )

2. In international trade, price terms such as CIF have nothing to do with the arrangement of insurance. (   )

3. Most carriers usually charge the same premium for the same coverage and the number of loss and damage claims. (   )

4. Insurance can be arranged directly with a wide variety of parties like a carrier, an insurer, an insurance broker, etc. (   )

5. Insurance for products such as dangerous goods and hazardous wastes is covered by the same insurance methods. (   )

Section 2 — A General Introduction to China's Cargo Insurance

In international buying and selling of goods, there are a number of risks. If they occur, it will involve traders in financial losses. For instance, cargoes in transit may be damaged due to breakage of packing, clash, fire, etc. These hazards, and many others, may be insured against loss and damage.

China Insurance Clauses are proposed by the People's Insurance Company of China (PICC). Established in 1949, PICC is a state-owned insurance company in China. It underwrites almost all kinds of insurance and has agents in almost all main ports and regions in the world.

According to PICC dated on January 1st, 1981, there are three basic risks in ocean cargo shipment: FPA, WA, and All Risks. However, some insurance applicants may find one of the three primary types of marine cargo insurance good enough for their shipment. The solution lies in extraneous risks which provide people with supplement choices. It falls into two kinds: General Additional Risks and Special Additional Risks.

General Additional Risks: The PICC can underwrite 11 kinds of general additional risks, they are: TPND (Theft, Pilferage and Non-delivery), Fresh Water and/or Rain Damage, Shortage, Leakage, Intermixture and Contamination, Clash and Breakage, Taint of Odor, Sweating and Heating, Hook Damage, Breakage of Packing, and Rust.

Special Additional Risks: Special additional risks are for the purpose of insuring total loss or partial loss of the insured goods due to special extraneous perils. There are eight kinds of special additional risks, including: Failure to Delivery, Import Duty, On Deck, Rejection, Aflatoxin, War, SRCC (Strike, Riots, Civil Commotions).

I. Read the passage and finish the mind-map of China's cargo insurance.

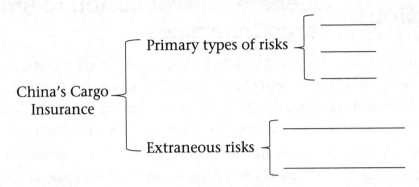

II. Match the terms in the left column with their translations in the right column.

1. 偷窃、提货不着险   A. Rust Risk

2. 淡水雨淋险   B. Taint of Odor Risk

3. 短量险   C. War Risk

4. 混杂和污损   D. Failure to Delivery Risk

5. 渗漏险   E. Breakage of Packing Risk

6. 碰损破碎险   F. Clash and Breakage Risks

7. 感染、串味险   G. Fresh Water and/or Rain Damage Risk

8. 受潮受热险   H. Import Duty Risk

9. 钩损险   I. SRCC (Strikes, Riots, Civil Commotions)

10. 锈损险   J. TPND (Theft, Pilferage and Non-delivery)

11. 包装破裂险   K. Leakage Risk

12. 战争险   L. Shortage Risk

13. 罢工、暴动、民变险   M. Hook Damage Risk

14. 拒受险   N. Sweating and Heating Damage

15. 进口关税险

O. Rejection Risk

16. 交货不着险

P. Intermixture and Contamination Risks

Part ② Case Study

In this part, you are supposed to read four letters on insurance.

Letter 1: Request for insurance arrangement

Situation: *Monika, a sales assistant from GML Porcelain Import Company Ltd., is writing a letter to ask her counterpart in China to effect insurance on behalf of her company for 110% of the invoice value against FPA for the account of GML.*

Dear Gabbie,

Subject: Your Sales Contract No. 900

We wish to draw your attention to your sales contract No. 900 covering 410 cartons of potteries, from which you will see that this order was placed on FOB basis.

As we now desire to have the shipment insured on your side, we shall appreciate it if you will kindly **effect insurance** on behalf of us against FPA **for 110% of the invoice value**, i.e., USD 6,200.

We shall of course **refund** the **premium** to you when you **draw on us** at sight **for** the amount requested, or, if you like, you can also send us your **debit note**.

Your approval of our request would be highly appreciated.

Yours faithfully,

Monika

Letter 2: Reply to an insurance request

Situation: *Gabbie, a sales assistant in Chaozhou Dinnerware Export Co. Ltd., has received a letter asking for effecting insurance for his business partner. In reply, he is writing a letter to confirm his arrangement of insurance.*

Dear Monika,

Subject: Our Sales Contract No. 900

We thank you for your letter of June 18th, requesting us to cover insurance on the goods under our S/C No. 900 **for your account**.

We are pleased to confirm having covered the above consignment with Ping'an Insurance Company of China Ltd. against FPA for 110% of the invoice value, i.e. USD 6,200. The **policy** will be sent to you in a day or two together with our debit note for the premium.

For your review, 410 cartons of potteries will be shipped on S/S "Dengfeng", sailing on or about the 8th next month.

We sincerely hope that we would have more cooperation in the future.

Best regards,

Gabbie

Letter 3: Request for extra insurance

Situation: *Jimmy, the buyer from a foreign trade company in India, writes a letter to the seller asking for effecting insurance to the inland city and adding extra insurance, i.e., 130% of the invoice value with the extra premium being borne on the buyer.*

Dear Judy,

Subject: Our Order No. MF701

We are pleased to inform you that we have concluded a transaction of 15,600 pieces of Christmas presents, from which you will certainly note that it is placed on CIF basis.

Please see to it that the punctual shipment of the goods is very important to catch the season. We would appreciate it if you could have the goods covered into the inland city to meet our customer's request. Moreover, we would like you to cover the goods against All Risks and WPA for 30% above the invoice value. We know that you usually effect insurance on the goods only for 110% of the invoice value. Therefore, the extra premium will **be borne on us**.

We sincerely hope that our request will meet with your approval and look forward to your early reply with keen interest.

Sincerely yours,

Jimmy

Letter 4: Reply to extra insurance requirement

Situation: *On receiving the buyer's request for effecting insurance to the inland city and adding extra insurance, the seller writes an email in reply and informs the buyer that he would accept to cover the insurance to the inland city, but he refuses to extend the coverage to 130% of the invoice value.*

Dear Jimmy,

Subject: Your Order No. MF701

In reply to your Order No. MF701 regarding insurance, we take the pleasure in informing you that your customer's request for insurance **coverage** up to the inland city is acceptable on condition that such extra premium is for your account.

However, we cannot grant you insurance coverage for 130% of the invoice value, because the contract stipulates that insurance is to be covered for 110% of invoice value. Besides, we have already signed on the insurance policy, any change of which will result in further trouble. Hope you will not think us **unaccommodating** as it has been settled.

We trust the above information serves your purpose. Meanwhile, we await your reply.

Sincerely yours,

Judy

Words and Expressions

1. **effect insurance** 办理保险

2. **for 110% of invoice value** 按发票金额的 110%

3. **refund** *v.* 退还

4. **premium** *n.* 保险费

5. **draw (a draft) on sb. for/against** 向某人开汇票索取

6. **debit note** 借方通知；索款通知单

7. **for your account** 由你方支付

8. **policy** *n.* 保险单

9. **be borne on sb.** 费用由……支付

10. **coverage** *n.* 承保范围；险别总称

11. **unaccommodating** *adj.* 不与人方便的，不通融的

Exercises

I. Match the sentences with the key points of letters on negotiating insurance arrangement and finish the table below.

1. We wish to refer you to your sales contract No. 900 for 410 cartons of potteries.

2. We hope you can insure the goods for 150% of the invoice value against All Risks instead of 110%.

3. We have covered the goods against All Risks and War Risk.

4. We shall of course refund the premium to you when you draw on us at sight for the amount requested, or, if you like, you can also send us your debit note.

5. We are pleased to confirm having covered the above consignment with Ping'an Insurance Company of China Ltd. against FPA for 110% of the invoice value, i.e., USD 6,200.

6. We thank you for your letter of September 30th, requesting us to effect insurance on the captioned shipment for your account.

7. If you want to add extra insurance, the premium should be on your side.

8. Please help us to cover the insurance as per the clause stipulated in the contract.

Key Points of Letters on Negotiating Insurance Arrangement	Sentences
Refer to previous contact	
Ask for arranging insurance	
Confirm effecting insurance	
Negotiate premium	

 II. Find the errors in the letter and improve it.

June 20th, 2022

Dear Sir,

Refer to our order No. A135 of 150 pieces of tea sets which is placed on FOB basis.

Therefore, you must get the shipment insured within the limited time. Please remember that the above-mentioned goods should be delivered before October 10th and the shipment should be made for Clash and Breakage Risks of 110% of the invoice value.

We sincerely hope that you can meet our request, or we may cancel the order.

Yours sincerely,

Jeff

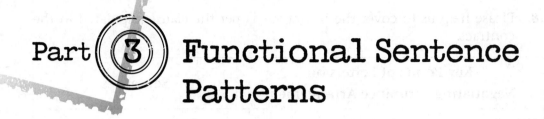

Part ③ Functional Sentence Patterns

1. Recalling Previous Contact

(1) We wish to refer you to our order No. 2501 for 850 sets of washing machines.

(2) We have received your letter of June 8th, asking us to cover the captioned order for 120% of the invoice value.

(3) We thank you for your letter of June 18th, requesting us to effect insurance on the captioned shipment for your account.

(4) In reply to your email of June 19th asking us to effect insurance on the above order, we are pleased to inform you that we have covered the shipment with PICC against WPA.

2. Asking for Arranging Insurance

(1) As per our previous negotiation, we would like to leave insurance arrangement to you.

(2) We shall be pleased if you could have the goods covered against All Risks on our behalf for 110% of the invoice value.

(3) We hope you can insure the goods for 150% of the invoice value against All Risks instead of 110%.

(4) Please help us to cover the insurance as per the clause stipulated in the contract.

3. Confirming Effecting Insurance

(1) We will arrange the insurance according to your request.

(2) For your information, we have taken out insurance with PICC against WPA for USD 4,500.

(3) We will have the captioned goods insured immediately under such circumstances to meet your requirements.

(4) We have already arranged insurance in compliance with your request.

4. Negotiating Premium

(1) TPND is not mentioned in the contract, so the premium should be on your side.

(2) Please see to it that you should be responsible for the premium if you extend the coverage.

(3) We hope that you can insure the goods for us, and the extra premium will be for our account.

(4) We wonder if you can do us a favor to arrange the insurance at our cost.

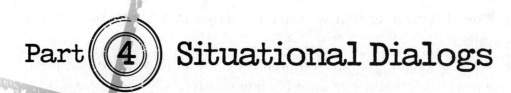

Part 4 Situational Dialogs

Dialog 1: *Monika, from California Import Co. Ltd., asked Li Han to handle the insurance of porcelain goods in Chaozhou on its behalf. They also talked about the types and rate of insurance.*

Monika: We wish to refer you to our order No. 254 for 3,260 pieces of porcelains. We would like you to help us with the insurance and we appreciate it very much.

Li Han: Yes, I see. Since our business is concluded on CIF, it would be our responsibility to cover the insurance on your behalf. What coverage would you like to take out on the goods?

Monika: Generally speaking, we only insure the goods against WPA.

Li Han: How about coverage other than WPA, for instance, Clash and Breakage Risks. You know, it is easy for porcelains to be broken.

Monika: Emm, sounds reasonable. OK, WPA and Clash and Breakage Risks.

Li Han: How about the insurance rate?

Monika: We would like to cover the goods for 110% of the invoice value. In addition, please see to it that the above-mentioned goods should be insured not later than June 30th.

Li Han: Please rest assured. We will handle the insurance as per your request.

Monika: Thanks a lot.

Li Han: You're welcome. When the policy is made, it will be sent to you immediately.

Dialog 2: *Jack, a salesman from an Indian foreign trade company, called Wen from Guangdong PDL Import and Export Co. Ltd., confirming the insurance rate.*

Jack: I'm calling to discuss the insurance rate you've requested for your order.

Wen: I see. I remember that we have requested 20% above the invoice value?

Jack: Yes, that's right. We have no problem conforming with your request, but we think that the amount is a bit excessive.

Wen: We've had a lot of trouble in the past with damaged goods.

Jack: I understand your concern. However, the normal rate for goods of this type is 110% of the total invoice amount.

Wen: We would feel more comfortable with the additional insurance coverage.

Jack: Unfortunately, if you want to expand the coverage, the extra premium should be on your side.

Wen: Was it not supposed to be included in the quotation?

Jack: Yes, but we quoted you normal coverage at regular rates.

Wen: I see. We hope that you can insure the goods for 20% plus the invoice value for us, and the extra premium will be for our account.

Jack: OK, we will arrange the insurance rate at your cost.

Wen: Thanks for your cooperation. We shall of course refund to you the extra premium upon receipt of your debit note or, if you like, you may draw on us at sight for the amount requested.

Exercise

Work in pairs and make a business dialog with your partner on arranging insurance according to the information given in the cue cards.

Cue Card A

You are Mr./Ms. Golden, the salesperson of an import company. You need to:

- refer to previous contact: concluding a transaction;
- ask for arranging insurance;
- require types of insurance and premium rate;
- show appreciation.

Cue Card B

You are Mr./Ms. Armstrong, the salesperson of an export company. You need to:

- confirm with appreciation;
- agree and ask for preference of insurance coverage;
- confirm insurance coverage;
- promise to effect insurance as requested.

Part 5 Skill Training

I. Match the words and phrases in the left column with their translations in the right column.

1. insurance coverage   A. 中国人民保险公司

2. All Risks   B. 水渍险

3. extra premium   C. 额外保险费

4. insurance policy   D. 保险范围，险种

5. PICC   E. 平安险

6. WPA   F. 一切险

7. FPA   G. 保险单

8. on or about   H. 被保人

9. be borne on sb.   I. 大约

10. the insured   J. 由······支付

II. Fill in the blanks with appropriate words given in the box.

covering	against	premium	coverage	insure
bear	prestige	covered	inconsistent	for

1. Please arrange insurance on the goods _____ All Risks.

2. The _____ rate for the shipment against WA is 0.7%.

3. If a higher percentage is required, we may do accordingly but you have to _____ the extra premium as well.

4. We usually effect insurance _____ 110% of the invoice value.

5. I'd like to have the insurance _____ for 130% of the invoice value.

6. We go through the L/C and find out the insurance clause is _____ with the practice.

7. Our products rank in front in the same field not only for the technological norm but also for the adoptability which brings our company high _____ in the line.

8. Please _____ the article against WPA.

9. We regret being unable to comply with your request for _____ insurance for 150% of the invoice value.

10. We can provide such additional _____ at a slightly higher premium.

III. Translate the following sentences into English or Chinese respectively.

1. 我公司可以承保海洋运输的所有险别。

2. 一切险的承保范围比平安险大。

3. 我们通常按发票金额的 110% 来投保。

4. 除水渍险和战争险外，请再投保破碎险。

5. 按照国际惯例，除非买方要求，我们通常不投保偷窃、提货不着险。

6. Insurance is to be covered by the sellers against All Risks for 110% of the invoice value with the PICC.

7. Please insure coverage at your end.

8. Please cover the insurance on the 300 sets of sewing machines under contract No. 345.

9. The rate of Risk of Breakage is 3%. If you prefer to cover it, the premium will be for your account.

10. If there is no definite direction from you, we'll effect insurance against WPA and War Risk.

IV. **Write a business letter according to the following situation.**

Miss Liao Wen is the manager of Ganjiang Potteries Ltd. who concluded a business deal with RTB Ornaments Ltd. for 1,500 tea sets. Write a letter for Liao Wen, asking the seller to cover insurance against FPA and Clash and Breakage on these fragile goods.

Part 6 Additional Reading

Insurance Policy

中国人民保险公司广州市分公司

The People's Insurance Company of China GUANGZHOU Branch

总公司设于北京   一九四九年创立

Head Office in Beijing   Established in 1949

货物运输保险单 CARGO TRANSPORTATION INSURANCE POLICY

发票号码（INVOICE NO.）NM134   保险单号次（POLICY NO.）PLC876

合同号（CONTRACT NO.）05MP561009   信用证号（L/C NO.）T-027651

被保险人（INSURED）GUANGDONG MACHINERY IMPORT AND EXPORT CORP.

中国人民保险有限公司（以下简称本公司）根据被保险人的要求，由被保险人向本公司缴付约定的保险费，按照本保险单承担险别和背面所载条款与下列特别条款承保下列货物运输保险，特立本保险单。

This policy of Insurance witnesses that the People's Insurance Company of China (hereinafter called "The Company"), at the request of the Insured and in consideration of the agreed premium paid to the company by the Insured, undertakes to insure the undermentioned goods in transportation subject to conditions of the Policy as per the Clauses printed overleaf and other special clauses attached hereon.

标记 Marks & No.s	包装及数量 Quantity	保险货物项目 Descriptions of Goods	保险金额 Amount Insured
F.V. ART No. = 9099 ROTTERDAM No.s: 1–1,000	1,000 CTNS 12,000 PCS	STAINLESS SCOOP	USD 126,720

总保险金额：

Total amount insured: SAY U.S. DOLLARS ONE HUNDRED TWENTY-SIX THOUSAND SEVEN HUNDRED AND TWENTY ONLY

保费　　　　　　　　　启运日期　　　　　　　　　载运输工具

Premium AS ARRANGED　　Date of shipment JUNE 20, 2022　　Per conveyance: Possession V16

自　　　　　　　　　　　经　　　　　　　　　　　至

From GUANGZHOU　　VIA _____　　To ROTTERDAM

承保险别：

Conditions: COVERING ALL RISKS AND WAR RISK FOR 110% INVOICE VALUE AS PER CIC DATED 1/1/1981

所保货物，如发生本保险单项下可能引起索赔的损失或损坏，应立即通知本公司下述代理人查勘。如有索赔，应向本公司提交保险单正本（本保险单共有　3　份正本）及有关文件。如一份正本已用于索赔，其余正本则自动失效。

In the event of loss or damage which may result in acclaim under this Policy, immediate notice must be given to the Company's Agent as mentioned here under. Claims, if any, one of the Original Policy which has been issued in ___three___ original(s) together with the relevant documents shall be surrendered to the Company. If one of the Original Policy has been accomplished, the others to be void.

中国人民保险公司广州市分公司

The People's Insurance Company of China GUANGZHOU Branch

赔款偿付地点：鹿特丹　　　　　　　授权签字：王天华

Claim payable at ROTTERDAM　　　　Authorized signature WANG TIANHUA

出单日期 2022 年 6 月 19 日

Issuing date JUNE 19, 2022

地址：中国广州黄河路 112 号　　　　　电话（TEL）：(020)86521049

Address: No. 112 Huanghe Road, Guangzhou, China　　传真（FAX）：(020)84404593

邮编（POST CODE）：510000

Chapter 10

Shipment

Learning Objectives

By completing this unit, students will learn:

- international transportation and bills of lading;
- how to analyze case letters on shipment;
- useful expressions and sentence patterns on shipment;
- how to negotiate on shipment.

Lead-in

Work in groups, discuss the following questions and then share your answers with the whole class.

1. Can you list some modes of shipment?

2. What are the features of ocean transport?

3. What are the steps of shipping arrangements?

4. How much do you know about bills of lading?

5. What constituents should be included when you write a letter on shipment?

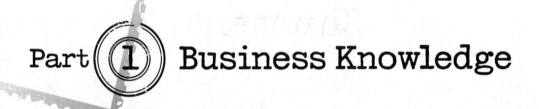

Part 1 Business Knowledge

Section 1 International Transportation of Goods

In international trade, transportation is one of the most important steps. Only through transportation can the goods be shipped from the seller's location to the buyer's location.

The fields in which foreign trade is involved are extensive, and the transportation lines are long. The links and procedures are numerous. This is because in international trade where an exporter and an importer are always far apart, the goods under the contract must go a long distance and sometimes change several carriers in transit before they reach the importer. In an international business, it is one of the basic tasks for the exporter to deliver the goods to the importer or carrier or agreed conveyance after the contract has been singed according to the stipulated time, place, and transport methods. Hence, the foreign traders must be equipped with fundamental knowledge of the international cargo transportation and shipment.

The delivery of goods means that the seller delivers the contract goods at the agreed time, place, and in the agreed manners to the buyer. In international sales of goods, the delivery also means to transfer the necessary documents at the stipulated time to the buyer.

As for the means of delivery in international practice, there are many methods to deliver the goods purchased, such as ocean transport, railway and road transport, air transport, river and lake transport, postal transport, pipeline transport, land bridge transport, international multimode transport and so on. Among these means of transport, ocean transport is the most widely used one with land transport second to it. The buyer and the seller can decide which method will be the best for the goods to be transported according to the goods' characteristics, quantity, transit journey, value, time, natural conditions and so on.

The procedure for arranging a shipment of goods can be complex. In such large firms as the Beijing World Trade Co. Ltd., a shipping department will take care of overseas shipping through close working connections with the China National Foreign Trade Transportation Corporation (Sinotrans) or the China Ocean Shipping Company (COSCO). In the smaller firms, this task is usually delegated, on a fee basis, to a freight forwarder, who can handle merchandise, documents, and information knowledgeably, efficiently, expeditiously, and honorably.

Exercises

I. Read the passage and choose the best answer to each question.

1. Why is transportation important in international trade?

A. It frequently occurs in international trade.

B. It helps to carry the goods to the buyer.

C. It is helpful for both the seller and the buyer.

D. It helps to execute the contract.

2. It can be concluded from the passage that transportation in international trade is complicated because of the following aspects EXCEPT that _____.

A. the goods under the contract must go a long distance

B. the goods under the contract sometimes change several carriers in transit

C. the exporter and the importer are always far apart

D. the fields involved in international transportation are very limited

3. According to the passage, the shipment clause should include the following aspects EXCEPT _____ .

A. carrier   B. stipulated time

C. stipulated place   D. transport methods

4. Which of the following statements is NOT true about the means of delivery?

A. There are many methods to deliver the goods purchased.

B. Ocean transport is the most widely used one.

C. The seller can decide which methods will be the best for the goods.

D. Several elements must be considered when choosing the means of delivery.

5. COSCO _____ .

A. has a close connection with big trading companies

B. is the biggest shipping company in China

C. is a freight forwarder

D. is a national trading corporation in Beijing

II. **Decide whether the statements are true (T) or false (F) according to the passage.**

1. In international trade, it is the exporter who is responsible for delivering the goods to the carrier. (   )

2. It is important that foreign traders should gain some fundamental knowledge about international transportation because of its complexity. (   )

3. Among the means of transport, ocean transport is the most widely used one with air transport second to it. (   )

4. The procedure for effecting a shipment of goods can be complicated. (   )

5. In large firms, the task of arranging shipment is usually delegated, on a fee basis, to a freight forwarder. (   )

Section 2 Bill of Lading

The most important document in shipping is the bill of lading signed by or on behalf of the transporter or the ship's master. Originally called a bill of lading, it is used to certify that the seller's goods have been received for transportation and delivery as stipulated. A bill of lading fulfills at least three important functions in international transportation trade.

- It is a receipt of goods indicating in what apparent order and conditions the goods have been received on board.

- It is a contract between the seller (shipper) and the shipping company (the carrier) for the transportation of the covered goods from the port of loading to stipulated port of destination.

- It is also a title document, evidence of ownership of the goods described and allows the legal owner of the bill of lading to transfer the goods at any time to any relevant party, for the owner of the bill of lading is also the owner of the goods. So when made out "to order", the bill of lading becomes in practice a negotiable instrument and is often used as security for loans and other purposes.

With the rapid development of international trade, transportation facilities have been greatly improved to meet the demands. To meet with the improvement, bills of lading that serve different methods of transportation appeared. There are ocean bill of lading (for shipment over an ocean), air waybill (for airplane), inland bill of lading (for inland surface transportation), and intermodal bill of lading. No matter how it is titled, a bill of lading is to convey ownership of the goods and to govern their transportation, but an air waybill is neither a document of title nor can it transfer ownership of the goods to which it refers.

To provide a solution to legal requirements of any national or local law, custom or practice requiring the contract of carriage to be evidenced in writing and signed, the Committee Maritime International (CMI) has adopted Rules for Electronic Bills of Lading. Under the Rules, upon receipt of goods, the carrier can send an electronic message to the shipper describing the goods, the contract terms, and a private key or code. The private key or code can be used to transfer shipper's rights to a third party. And the third party then becomes a new holder. The carrier then cancels the original key and gives a new key to the new person entitled to control of the goods. In this way, the key holder should have the same rights as the bill of lading holder.

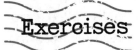

I. Read the passage and answer the following questions.

1. What are the functions of a bill of lading?

_____

2. How many types of bills of lading are there in international trade? What are they?

_____

3. How much do you know about the air waybill?

_____

4. What does CMI do to meet the requirements internationally on the contract of carriage?

_____

5. How can the carrier transfer the shipper's rights to a third party?

_____

II. Match the words and phrases in the left column with their translations in the middle column and definitions in the right column.

1. transporter   A. 托运人   a. a mode of transport involving two or more different ways of transport

2. master   B. 运输公司   b. the seller that sends something by ship, road, train, or air

3. negotiable instrument   C. 航空运单   c. a company that moves goods from one place to another

4. air waybill   D. 海运提单   d. a bill used for inland surface transportation

5. inland bill of lading   E. 可转让的票据   e. someone who is in charge of a ship

6. ocean bill of lading   F. 多式联运的   f. a bill used for shipment over an ocean

7. intermodal   G. 陆运提单   g. a document that can be transferred

8. shipper   H. 船长   h. a bill used for airplane transport

Part ② Case Study

In this part, you are supposed to read four letters on shipment.

Letter 1: Urging shipment

Situation: *Melbourne Import Company Ltd. has placed an order for 15,000 pieces of backpacks. Lynn, a sales assistant in the company, is writing a letter to Guangzhou Export Fabric Ltd. to emphasize the importance of punctual shipment and urge them to dispatch the goods with the least possible delay.*

Dear Sirs,

We are glad that we have concluded a transaction of 15,000 pieces of backpacks.

According to the stipulation of our contract, the shipment **is supposed to** be effected by August 12th, 2022. However, up to this moment we have not received any information concerning this lot. We would like to remind you that goods should be shipped punctually.

As the **selling season** is approaching, we shall appreciate it very much if you ship the goods **scheduled to** sail on or about August 5th, thus enabling the goods to catch the **brisk demand** at the start of the season. Therefore, please **do your utmost to get the goods dispatched** with the least possible delay.

Thank you for your cooperation in advance.

Yours faithfully,

Lynn

Letter 2: Shipping advice

Situation: *In reply to Lynn's letter of urging shipment, Jackie, a sales assistant from Guangzhou Export Fabric Ltd., informs her that the goods will be shipped today and scheduled to arrive at the destination on or about August 20th.*

Dear Lynn,

We are pleased to advise you that the backpacks you ordered will be dispatched by S/S "Five Star" today from our port to Melbourne at your request, i.e., August 5th, and they are **due to arrive** at the destination on or about August 20th.

In spite of great care in packing, it sometimes may happen that a few packages are broken in transit. Should there be any breakages or other complaints, please do not hesitate to let us know.

Further details concerning the consignment including packing and shipping marks are contained in our invoice No. 658 enclosed in triplicate. In order to cover this shipment, we have drawn on you a draft under L/C to be negotiated through any bank in China, with relative **shipping documents**.

We trust that the goods will reach you in good condition and give you complete satisfaction.

Yours faithfully,

Jackie

Letter 3: Giving shipping instructions

Situation: *In reply to the letter urging opening the L/C, Shelia informs the buyer that the L/C was established through the JEF Bank, Toronto on July 30th. Meanwhile, she also gives the seller some shipping instructions.*

Dear Sirs,

In reply to your letter dated August 10th, we are pleased to advise that the confirmed, irrevocable letter of credit No. 567 for the amount of USD 87,000 was established through the JEF Bank, Toronto on July 30th.

Upon receipt of the L/C, please deliver our order No. ET901 for men's shirts per **M/V** "Fabulous", **ETA** at Toronto on or about September 5th, and confirm by return that the goods will be ready in time.

We also ask you to see to it that all the goods are well packed, so as to avoid damage in transit. We shall appreciate your close cooperation in this respect.

We are looking forward to your early shipment.

Yours faithfully,

Shelia

Letter 4: Asking for transshipment

Situation: *With reference to the buyer's letter giving shipping instructions, Rebecia writes a letter to the buyer asking for transshipment because of few direct liners to the port of destination and suggests transshipment via Hong Kong.*

Dear Sirs,

Subject: Order No. ET901

We have got your letter of August 12th, giving us the specific shipping instructions on the above-mentioned goods.

As the M/Vs to the port of destination are few and far between, we are still waiting for a reply from the **shipping company** concerning the matter of space. To be frank with you, we have some difficulties in obtaining **shipping space**. We hope you can understand our position and we are doing our utmost to deliver the goods before the relative credit expires. We expect to give you the result of our efforts by email as soon as possible.

An **alternative** is to ship the goods by transshipment. If you allow us to transship via Hong Kong, we assure you that the shipment will reach your port in time. In that case, the L/C shall be amended accordingly.

Please send us your reply at your earliest convenience.

Yours faithfully,

Rebecia

Words and Expressions

1. **be supposed to** 应该

2. **selling season** 销售旺季

3. **scheduled to...** 预计……

4. **brisk demand** 旺盛的需求

5. **do one's utmost to...** 尽某人的最大努力……

6. **get the goods dispatched** 发货

7. **due to arrive** 预计到达

8. **shipping document** 装运单据

9. **M/V = motor vessel** 轮船

10. **ETA = estimated time of arrival** 预计抵达时间

11. **shipping company** 运输公司

12. **shipping space** 舱位

13. **alternative** *n.* 另一选择

Exercises

I. **Match the sentences with the key points of letters on shipment and finish the table below.**

1. As the busy season is approaching, we would appreciate it if you could deliver the goods on time.

2. In accordance with the contract, please see to it that the goods are to be shipped from your city to our port by the end of this month.

3. The shipment under contract No. 436 has been effected by M.V. "Helpful", which is scheduled to arrive at your city next month.

4. As our users are in urgent need of the consignment, please get the goods dispatched within the stipulated time.

5. We have pleasure in notifying you that we have shipped the goods today by S.S. "Yue". They are to be transshipped at Singapore and are expected to reach your port early next month.

6. As there is no direct liner to the destination, please allow transshipment.

7. Please ship the first lot under contract No. 247 by S.S. "Tiger" scheduled to sail on or about March 8th.

8. In compliance with your request, we have to arrange transshipment.

Key Points of Letters on Shipment	Sentences
Give shipping instructions	
Urge to ship promptly	
Give shipping advice	
Ask for transshipment or partial shipment	

II. Find the errors in the letter and improve it.

August 10th, 2022

Dear Sir,

Because there is no direct vessel to your port, we will postpone the delivery.

We take pleasure in advise you that we will ship the goods in contract tomorrow. Since our customers are in urgent need of the goods, if you arrange the shipment as soon as possible, we will be delighted.

In spite of our again and again complaints, we have got the reply on shipping.

We would highly appreciated if you would accept our suggestions.

Yours sincerely,

Jellie

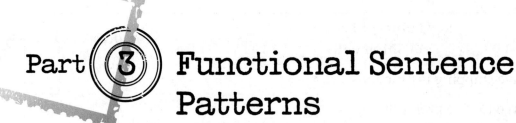

Part ③ Functional Sentence Patterns

1. Urging Shipment

(1) Since our customers are in urgent need of the goods, please arrange the shipment as soon as possible.

(2) We shall appreciate it if you would manage to advance the shipment.

(3) As the busy season is approaching, we would appreciate it if you could deliver the goods on time.

(4) Till today we haven't got the goods we ordered under the contract No. 9806. Please make the shipment immediately.

(5) I wonder if it is possible for you to effect shipment in March.

2. Giving Shipping Instructions

(1) For the goods under our contract No. 2208, please book space on S.S. "May", which is due to arrive at our port on or about March 20th.

(2) Please ship the first lot under contract No. 1170 by S.S. "Tiger" scheduled to sail on or about March 8th.

(3) As the market is declining, please postpone the shipment of our ordered goods to May.

(4) May I know if you are in a position to make shipment by the middle of March?

(5) Your shipment should be effected in two equal monthly lots during May and June.

3. Giving Shipping Advice

(1) We advise you that the intelligent toys you ordered in September will be effected by S.S. "Flexible" next Tuesday.

(2) The remainder of the goods will be shipped in early December.

(3) We are pleased to confirm you that your order for 2,000 sheets of Indian Rugs will be shipped on June 15th by "Victoria" in compliance with the stipulation set forth in the L/C.

(4) We have pleasure in advising you that we will ship the goods under Contract No. 385 in June, to be more exact, June 22nd.

(5) We have pleasure in notifying you that we have shipped today by S.S. "Yue" 2,000 pairs of shoes. They are to be transshipped at Hong Kong and are expected to reach your port early next month.

4. Asking for Transshipment or Partial Shipment

(1) As there is no direct liner to the destination, please allow transshipment.

(2) According to the shipping documents, transshipment and partial shipment are permitted.

(3) If transshipment is allowed, the port of transshipment is marked.

(4) In compliance with your request, we have to arrange transshipment.

(5) The container was off-loaded by the shipping company at Busan, so we have to transship.

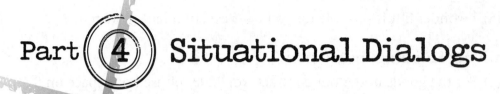

Part 4 Situational Dialogs

Dialog 1: *Kelly has placed an order with Canton Best Print Company for 7,250 pieces of Christmas presents. However, she has not got the delivery information yet. Therefore, she calls Jackie from Canton Best Print Company, urging him to deliver the goods as soon as possible.*

Kelly: Hi, good morning, this is Kelly. We haven't got any delivery information for our goods. We are desirous to know when you can effect the shipment.

Jackie: I am sorry we cannot effect shipment right now.

Kelly: Then, when is the earliest date we can expect the shipment?

Jackie: By the middle of September, I think.

Kelly: That would be too late. October is the peak season for this commodity in our market. So, you must deliver the goods before the end of August, otherwise we won't be able to catch the selling season. You know, it takes about one month to reach our port.

Jackie: I would be glad to do that if we can. However, I am sorry that our factories have rush orders on hand and are busy getting the goods ready, making out the documents, and booking the shipping space… all this takes time. So, I'm afraid it's difficult to improve any further on the time.

Kelly: Can't you find some way for an earlier delivery? If you can't effect the delivery by the end of August, we shall keep the right to terminate the contract.

Jackie: All right, we'll do our best to advance the shipment.

Kelly: Thank you very much for your cooperation.

Dialog 2: *Canton Best Print Company has shipped the goods ordered by Kelly. So, Jackie calls her and gives her the shipping advice.*

Jackie: We have pleasure in notifying you that we have shipped your goods today by S.S. "Yue".

Kelly: Thanks a lot. What is the estimated date of arrival?

Jackie: They are to be transshipped at Hong Kong and are expected to reach your port by the end of September.

Kelly: I see, then we can catch the peak season in October.

Jackie: I am glad to hear that. In order to assure you of the goods reaching you in good condition, all of them were packed in special containers.

Kelly: You are so considerate. We'd unpack and examine them immediately on arrival.

Jackie: Do not hesitate to notify us if any damage to the goods occurred in transit.

Kelly: Em, I hope everything goes well. How about the shipping documents?

Jackie: We'll email you one set of shipping documents covering this shipment later.

Kelly: Could you tell us what these documents are?

Jackie: Of course, one copy of non-negotiable bill of lading, one copy of commercial invoice, one copy of certificate of origin, one copy of certificate of quality, one copy of packing list, one copy of insurance policy, and one copy of survey report.

Kelly: Thanks. We hope this consignment will reach us in time and in good order.

Exercise

Work in pairs and make a business dialog with your partner on shipment according to the information given in the cue cards.

Cue Card A

You are Mr./Ms. Lion, the salesperson of an import company. You need to:

- inform the establishment of L/C;
- urge prompt shipment;
- emphasize the importance of punctual shipment;
- show thanks for cooperation.

Cue Card B

> You are Mr./Ms. Wheat, the salesperson of an export company. You need to:
> - show appreciation and confirm the receipt of L/C;
> - promise to effect shipment as early as possible;
> - confirm the date of shipment;
> - expect further transaction.

Part ⑤ Skill Training

I. **Fill in the blanks with proper prepositions.**

1. All the products shall cater _____ the requirements of the customers.

2. Any delay _____ shipment will cause us unexpected expenses.

3. The goods _____ question will be shipped on board S.S. "Merry Captain" soon.

4. Please send the goods needed in time so that we can put them _____ the market.

5. The seller shall compensate _____ all the losses incurred owing to the negligence before delivery.

6. Please fulfill the order _____ earliest convenience.

7. We are involved _____ no small difficulties.

8. We may inform you all the time of the development _____ our end.

9. We have some difficulty _____ obtaining the import license.

10. If you allow transshipment _____ Hong Kong, you can get the goods in time.

II. **Fill in the blanks with the proper forms of the words given in the box. The words can be used more than once.**

ship	transship	compensate	schedule

1. We have booked _____ space for your order No. 475.

2. The seller shall _____ for any damage to the goods before delivery.

3. As there is no direct liner to your port from Qingdao, the goods have to be _____ at Hong Kong.

4. Please ship the goods under the captioned contract No. 826 by M/V Yueshun _____ to sail on or about August 26th.

5. We shall accept your order on condition that the goods are shipped on board per direct steamer without _____.

6. You should refer to the shipping company for _____.

7. The _____ company will be responsible for the damage in transit.

8. The time of _____ is at your option and the goods will be shipped in one lot.

III. **Choose the best answer to complete each of the following sentences.**

1. In our letter of May 5, we made _____ clear that shipment is to be effected in June.

   A. you   B. them

   C. that   D. it

2. According to the shipping _____, it will be impossible for us to ship the goods in October.

   A. schedule   B. mark

   C. document   D. notice

3. You now wish to advance the date of shipment _____ one month.

   A. at   B. to

   C. for   D. by

4. Please note that the goods you ordered can certainly be shipped immediately _____ receipt of your L/C.

   A. in   B. on

   C. at   D. before

5. As we are one of the leading importers in this line, we are _____ to transport the goods in one lot.

   A. at a position   B. of a position

   C. on a position   D. in a position

6. We are confident that the package of our products will _____ the roughest handling in transit.

    A. suffer from   B. stand up to

    C. stand to   D. put up

7. In compliance with your request, we have to _____ transshipment.

    A. arrange   B. do

    C. affect   D. advance

8. The shipment time is in June or July at our _____ and the goods will be shipped in one _____.

    A. choice; shipment   B. option; lot

    C. decision; cargo   D. option; consign

9. It is difficult to reserve _____ space on account of heavy congestion.

    A. shipment   B. shipping

    C. shipped   D. ship

10. We shall appreciate _____ if you would manage to advance the shipment.

    A. it   B. them

    C. that   D. those

IV. Translate the following sentences into English or Chinese respectively.

1. 很抱歉我们无法在半个月内发货，因为停靠我方港口的班轮很少。

2. 装运方面的任何延误都会给我们带来不便。

3. 销售季节日益临近，但我方还未收到任何关于装船的消息。

4. 根据合同规定，由于运输延迟而造成的损失由你方赔偿。

5. 由于这批货物涉及数量大，请尽力安排装运。

6. We will ship the goods immediately so that you can put the goods on the market.

7. The goods we dispatched to you will cater for the requirements of your customers.

8. We haven't received any news about shipment of 3,000 sets of color TV under contracts No. E493 and No. 2864, which involves us in big trouble.

9. As the steamers to your port are few and far between, it is difficult for us to book shipping space on a direct liner.

10. We are informed by ABC Shipping Company that S.S. "Winter" is due to sail from your city to our port on or about 6th this month.

(V.) Write a business letter according to the following situation.

You have concluded a transaction of ginseng with a Korean businessman on FOB basis. Now write a letter to give shipping instructions and packing details as follows:

- confirm the transaction and inform the seller of the shipping space booked;

- ask the seller to contact the shipping company;

- give instructions for shipping marks;

- expect prompt shipment.

Part (6) Additional Reading

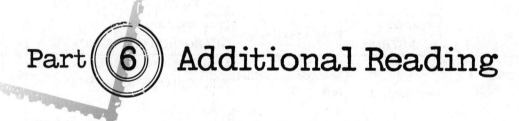

Bill of Lading

Shipper ABC COMPANY NO. 128 ZHOUSHAN XILU ROAD, GUANGDONG		B/L No. 中 国 外 运 广 东 公 司 SINOTRANS GUANGDONG COMPANY **OCEAN BILL OF LADING**
Consignee or order TO ORDER OF UFJ BANK, TOKYO		SHIPPED on board in apparent good order and condition (unless otherwise indicated) the goods or packages specified herein and to be discharged at the mentioned port of discharge or as near thereto as the vessel may safely get and be always afloat.
Notify address XYZ COMPANY, 6–2 OHTEMACHI,1–CHOME, CHIYADA-KU, TOKYO		
Pre-carriage by	Port of loading GUANGZHOU	The weight, measurement, marks and numbers, quality, contents and value, being particulars furnished by the Shipper, are not checked by the Carrier on loading.
Vessel VICTORY V.666	Port of transshipment	

(Continued)

Port of discharge TOKYO	Final destination KYOTO	The Shipper, Consignee and the Holder of this Bill of Lading hereby expressly accept and agree to all printed, written or stamped provisions, exceptions and conditions of this Bill of Lading, including those on the back hereof. IN WITNESS whereof the number of original Bills of Lading stated below have been signed, one of which being accomplished the other(s) to be void.		
Container seal No. or marks and No.s	Number and kind of package	Description of goods	Gross weight (kgs.)	Measurement (m³)
XYZ TOKYO 04GD002 1–88 CTNS SEAL NO. 006789	PACKED IN 88 CARTONS. SHIPPED IN ONE CONTAINER.	HOSPITAL UNIFORM 5,250 PCS	1,232.00 KGS	4.20 CBM

Freight and charges FREIGHT PREPAID			REGARDING TRANSSHIPMENT INFORMATION PLEASE CONTACT	
Ex. rate	Prepaid at GUANGZHOU	Freight payable at	Place and date of issue GUANGZHOU JAN. 18, 2022	
	Total prepaid	Number of original Bs/L 3/3	Signed for or on behalf of the Master PERFECT LOGISTICS COMPANY 陈　伟 As Agent	

Chapter 11

Complaints and Claims

Learning Objectives

By completing this unit, students will learn:

- common causes of complaints and claims in international trade;
- how to analyze case letters on complaints and claims;
- useful expressions and sentence patterns related to complaints and claims;
- how to handle complaints and claims.

Lead-in

Work in groups, discuss the following questions and then share your answers with the whole class.

1. What are complaints and claims?

2. Under what circumstances would the buyer make complaints or claims against the seller?

3. What are the strategies for making complaints or claims?

4. How can you deal with written complaints or claims in business?

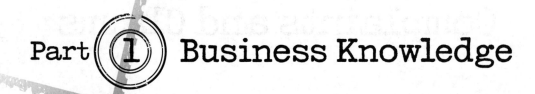

Part ① Business Knowledge

Section 1 Complaints and Claims

In foreign trade, it is ideal that the seller delivers the goods conforming to the contract in respect of quality, specification, quantity, and packing, and hands over the documents concerning the goods at the right time and place stipulated in the contract. And the buyer makes payment for the goods and takes delivery of them in the same manner specified in the contract. However, there always exists a gap between ideal and reality. Complaints or claims may sometimes arise in spite of the well-planned and careful work in the performance of a sales contract. In practice, it is not infrequent that the exporter or the importer neglects or fails to perform any of his or her obligations, thus giving rise to breach of contract and various trade disputes, which, subsequently, lead to claim, arbitration, or even litigation.

Breach of a contract means the refusal or failure by a party of a contract to fulfill an obligation imposed on him under that contract, resulting from, e.g., repudiation of liability before completion, or conduct preventing proper performance.

There are two kinds of complaints or claims made by buyers.

The first kind is a genuine complaint or claim, which arises from such situations as the following:

- The wrong goods may have been delivered.
- The quality may not be satisfactory.
- The shipment may have been found damaged, short or late.

The second kind is a false complaint or claim, which is made by buyers who find fault with the goods as an excuse to escape from the contract, because they no longer want the goods or because they have found that they can buy them cheaper elsewhere.

Suppose you are the buyer and are suffering from someone's mistake. If a complaint or claim has to be made, the matter should be investigated in detail and these details should be laid before the party charged. Sometimes, a reference to the previously satisfactory deliveries and services may help to win more sympathetic consideration of the present complaint or claim. You must handle complaints or claims in accordance with the principle of "on the first ground to our advantage and with restraint" and settle them amicably to the satisfaction of all parties concerned. It is necessary to study the case in question and ascertain what the real cause is and who is the party to be held responsible. You must also be careful in choosing the wording in your correspondence so as to avoid any misunderstandings.

Exercises

I. Read the passage and choose the best answer to each question.

1. Which statement is NOT true according to the first paragraph?

A. Complaints may arise when one party fails to execute the contract in respect of quality, specification, quantity, and packing, and documents.

B. With well-planned and careful work in the performance of a sales contract, complaints or claims can never arise.

C. Complaints may occur when the exporter or the importer neglects or fails to perform any of his or her obligations.

D. When complaints are not solved appropriately, they may subsequently lead to claim, arbitration, or even litigation.

2. According to the passage, which is NOT the situation in which complaints may arise?

A. The wrong name of the importer was in the contract.

B. The wrong goods may have been delivered.

C. The quality may not be satisfactory.

D. The shipment may have been found damaged, short or late.

3. What may be the main reason for a false complaint?

A. Quality of the goods.

B. Quantity of the goods.

C. Size of the goods.

D. Price of the goods.

4. If a complaint or claim has to be made, what should you do about it?

A. The matter should not be investigated in detail.

B. The investigated details should be laid after the party charged.

C. You may refer to the previously satisfactory deliveries and services to win more sympathetic consideration.

D. You may turn to arbitration or even litigation directly.

5. Which of the following is NOT mentioned as a way of handling complaints and claims reasonably?

A. To be in accordance with the principle of "on the first ground to our advantage and with restraint".

B. To settle them amicably to the satisfaction of all parties concerned.

C. To blame the party who is responsible and ask for claims.

D. To choose the right wording carefully in the correspondence.

II. **Decide whether the statements are true (T) or false (F) according to the passage.**

1. In foreign trade, it is always the case that the seller delivers the goods conforming to the contract and the buyer makes payment for the goods and takes delivery of them. (   )

2. Complaints or claims may sometimes arise despite well-planned and careful work in the performance of a sales contract. (   )

3. Breach of a contract means the refusal or failure by a party of a contract to fulfill an obligation imposed on him under that contract. (   )

4. A genuine complaint is possible when the buyer no longer wants the goods. (   )

5. If a complaint or claim arises, making an apology to the other party is the first step for the further smooth cooperation. (   )

Section 2 How to Handle Complaints and Claims

A claim is a demand or a request made by buyers or sellers for correction of faults or troubles occurring in international trade. In the process of fulfilling a contract or thereafter and when there are trade disputes between the buyer and the seller, complaints or even claims will possibly arise. In such circumstances, the party who lodges a complaint or a claim should be professional, skillful, and polite. Meanwhile, the party who receives the complaint or claim should pay serious attention to that, make an active adjustment with professional knowledge of international business, and make a timely reply. In general, it is advisable for both the seller and the buyer to properly settle the disputes through amicable negotiation rather than through arbitration or by law. However, complaints or claims are not the inevitable results of doing international business. In fact, when there are no disputes between the buyer and the seller in trade, shipping advice will be the final document sent by the seller in a transaction.

Complaints from customers are bound to happen to any business owner from time to time no matter how the company's policies and customer service may be.

These occurrences are not all bad. In fact, they provide a great opportunity to enhance the relationship with your customer.

If your customer complains in an oral way, follow these steps for a great outcome.

- Listen fully to the complaint without interrupting or defending yourself or your company.
- Validate the customer's feelings.
- Repeat what you heard as the problem.
- Ask the customer what he or she would like to see as the solution.

- Repeat the desired solution. Ask if you have captured it accurately.

- Tell them what you will do to resolve the situation. Ask if the proposed solution is satisfactory.

- When you get to the desired solution, thank them for their candor and tell them what you will do.

- Do it.

- Contact the client and ask if the solution was satisfactory.

- Ask if you can post the experience and if they will comment on the fact that the customer service was good.

We all make mistakes, but what makes us different is how we handle them.

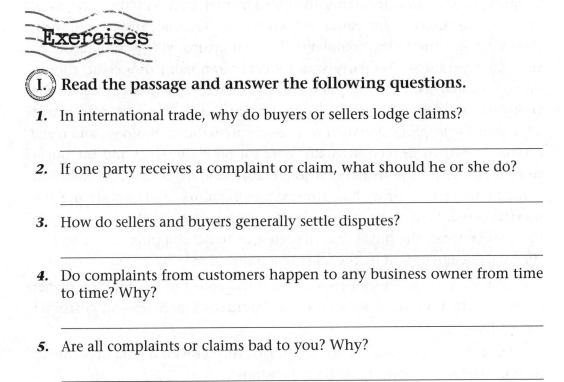

Exercises

I. Read the passage and answer the following questions.

1. In international trade, why do buyers or sellers lodge claims?

_____

2. If one party receives a complaint or claim, what should he or she do?

_____

3. How do sellers and buyers generally settle disputes?

_____

4. Do complaints from customers happen to any business owner from time to time? Why?

_____

5. Are all complaints or claims bad to you? Why?

_____

II. Translate the following sentences into Chinese.

1. In the process of fulfilling a contract or thereafter and when there are trade disputes between the buyer and the seller, complaints or even claims will possibly arise.

2. In general, it is advisable for both the seller and the buyer to properly settle the disputes through amicable negotiation rather than through arbitration or by law.

3. In fact, when there are no disputes between the buyer and the seller in trade, shipping advice will be the final document sent by the seller in a transaction.

4. Listen fully to the complaint without interrupting or defending yourself or your company.

5. When you get to the desired solution, thank them for their candor and tell them what you will do.

Part 2 Case Study

In this part, you are supposed to read four letters on complaints.

Letter 1: Lodging a claim

Situation: *Guangzhou Mascube Co. Ltd. has imported 4,500 vacuum cleaners from BRK Germany. After checking the goods, they found that several vacuum cleaners were seriously damaged, so they lodge a claim for the loss.*

Dear Sirs,

We duly received your documents and took delivery of the vacuum cleaners on arrival in Guangzhou.

We are much obliged to you for the prompt execution of this order. Everything appeared right and in good condition until we opened the cases and examined the contents. Unfortunately, it was found that cases No. 5 and No. 8 were broken and several vacuum cleaners inside them were seriously damaged.

We have had the cases and contents examined by the **insurance surveyor** but, as you will see from the enclosed copy of the report, he maintains that the damage was due to insecure packing and not to an unduly rough handling of the cases. We, therefore, have to **lodge a claim** against you for the loss of $3,000 we have sustained.

We are looking forward to your early reply to this matter.

Yours faithfully,

Aidan Lee

Letter 2: Explaining the reasons of the damage

Situation: *After checking the documents and procedures carefully, BRK Germany writes to Guangzhou Mascube Co. Ltd., indicating that the damage is not their fault, but the fault of the shipping company.*

Dear Aidan,

Thank you for your letter of September 15th and we are pleased to know that the consignment was delivered promptly, but it was with great regret that several vacuum cleaners in cases No. 5 and No. 8 were damaged, as mentioned in your letter.

You may be aware that our cleaners have been sold in a number of markets abroad for quite a long time, and all our customers have been satisfied with our packing. Every shipment of our export is strictly inspected by our shipping department before loading, and each packing is subject to careful examination. The goods under the above order were in perfect condition when they were shipped, and individual cases were clearly marked with "HANDLE WITH CARE", "FRAGILE", and other necessary warning and indicative marks. The clean B/L supports these facts.

After **going into the matter** carefully, we presume that the damage might be due to rough handling in transit or during unloading.

Your claim should be referred to the shipping company or the insurance company as a "**mishap**".

Yours faithfully,

Douglas

Letter 3: Asking the reasons of delay

Situation: *Guangzhou Baolite Company Ltd. placed an order with Rothy's Company Ltd., but didn't receive the goods as stipulated in the contract, so Guangzhou Baolite Company Ltd. complains it to Rothy's Company and asks the reasons of delay.*

Dear Sirs,

When we placed our order for men's shoes on August 12th, we did so on the understanding that delivery could be finished by September 15th. We are surprised that we have not yet received the goods or any news from you as to when we can expect the delivery.

As the time for shipment is now **considerably overdue**, we are really disappointed and should be obliged by your informing us of the reason for the delay.

This is the first time in many years that we have had to complain and we expect that you will look into the matter at once.

We hope that you will do your utmost to ensure that our consignment arrives soon.

Look forward to your earliest reply.

Sincerely yours,

Michael Wang

Letter 4: Making an apology

Situation: *After receiving the complaint letter from Guangzhou Baolite Company Ltd., Rothy's Company Ltd. looked into the reasons immediately and found that the delay was due to the forwarder. Now they make an apology, promising the arrival of goods within 10 days.*

Dear Mr. Wang,

We have received your letter dated September 20th, and hope you will accept our apologies for the delay in sending your order for men's shoes which should have been finished by September 15th.

The goods are in fact still with the **forwarder**. We assure you that your order has been attended with care, and the forwarder has been instructed to treat your shipment with absolute priority. Furthermore, we are given to understand that dispatch will be effected by S.S. "Champion", due to arrive in Guangzhou on or about September 30th.

We greatly regret the annoyance caused by the delayed delivery of your order. We could put forward some excuse, but we **refrain from** doing so because our mistake is not **pardonable**.

We are terribly sorry for the trouble caused by the error and wish to assure you that extra care will be taken in the execution of your further orders.

Yours faithfully,

Rothy

Words and Expressions

1. **insurance surveyor** 保险检查员

2. **lodge a claim** 索赔

3. **go into the matter** 调查此事

4. **mishap** *n.* 小事故

5. **considerably** *adv.* 非常，很；相当多地

6. **overdue** *adj.* 逾期的，过期的

7. **forwarder** *n.* 货运代理

8. **refrain from** 克制，忍住；抑制

9. **pardonable** *adj.* 可原谅的

Exercises

I. Match the sentences with the key points of letters on complaints and claims and finish the table below.

1. We will appreciate it if you could look into the matter, and let us know your disposal.

2. Unfortunately it was found that case No. 5 was broken and several dozens of thermos inside them were seriously damaged.

3. We duly received your documents and took delivery of the goods on arrival in Guangzhou.

4. We regret to inform you that the goods forwarded to us are in unsatisfactory state.

5. We, therefore, have to lodge a claim against you for the loss of $3,000 we have sustained.

6. As we need the articles we ordered to complete deliveries to our own customers, we must ask you to arrange the dispatch of replacements at once.

Key Points of Letters on Complaints and Claims	Sentences
Mention the need to complain	
Confirm receipt of the goods	
State your reason for being dissatisfied and ask for explanation	
Refer to the inconvenience caused	
Suggest how the matter should be put right	

II. Match the sentences with the key points of letters on replying to complaints and claims and finish the table below.

1. We are sorry for the trouble caused by the error and wish to assure you that care will be taken in the execution of your further orders.

2. We have received your email of...complaining about...

3. After going into the matter carefully, we presume that the damage might be due to rough handling in transit or during unloading.

4. In the survey report, we find out that...

5. It was with great regret that we heard that several thermoses in case No. 5 were damaged, as mentioned in your letter.

6. We apologize for causing you a good deal of inconvenience.

Key Points of Letters on Replying to Complaints and Claims	Sentences
Confirm receipt of the complaint	
Show regret for the damaged goods	
Explain the case	
Show apology and ensure future attention	

III. **Find the errors in the letter and improve it.**

November 15th, 2022

Dear Sirs,

Thank you for your letter. We were glad to know that the consignment was delivered promptly, but it was with great regret that we heard the case did not have the goods.

We find that a mistake was indeed made and we have arranged for the right goods to be dispatched to you at once. Relative documents will be mailed too.

You may expect to receive the goods soon.

We apologize the inconvenience you have sustained. Sorry again!

Yours faithfully,

Edison

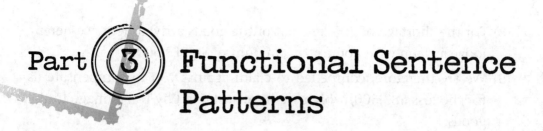

Part 3 Functional Sentence Patterns

1. Making Complaints

(1) We are writing to complain about the shipment of our order No. 132 for TV sets received today.

(2) We inform you with regret that recently there are quite many complaints from our customers about your men's shirts.

(3) We have to complain to you about the delay in shipment which has caused us much trouble.

(4) We regret to have to complain about the late delivery of the goods under our order No. 133.

(5) This being the case, we have to lodge a complaint against you for the inferior quality.

2. Reasons for Complaints

(1) You have confirmed our order, but to our surprise, we have not yet received the goods or any advice from you when we may expect delivery.

(2) After checking the goods against your invoice, we discovered a considerable shortage in number.

(3) We are very much surprised at the news that 12 pieces of fur were found missing without the cases showing any sign of being tampered with.

(4) We are unable to accept the shipments today, as they had been completely smashed when they reached us.

(5) After examining the curtain materials supplied under our order No. 234, we must express our disappointment at their quality.

3. Asking for Claims

(1) Based on the survey report, we hereby lodge our claim against you for the 60 cartons short delivered.

(2) For the shortage of 200 kgs. out of the goods arrived here, we hereby lodge a claim with you for the amount of Stg. £3,500.

(3) We are therefore, compelled to claim against you to compensate us for the loss $83,500, which we have sustained by the damage to the goods.

(4) We must ask you to replace them with good salable ones.

(5) As much of this consignment will be practically useless, kindly allow me a liberal discount upon the price agreed upon.

4. Showing Expectation

(1) We hope you will settle this matter and bring the case to a satisfactory close. We trust that there will be no repetition of this kind of trouble.

(2) We would like you to inform us of what you decide to do regarding our losses. We hope you will eventually take into consideration our future business relations and let us have your remittance in due course.

(3) We feel sure that you will give our claims your most favorable consideration and let us have your settlement at an early date. Your early explanation of this discrepancy will be appreciated.

(4) Of course, we prefer to settle the claim by amicable means instead of resorting to arbitration.

(5) This is the first time in many years that we have had to complain and we expect that you will look into the matter at once.

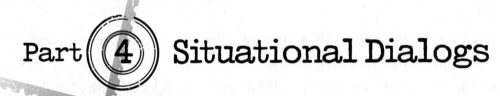

Part ④ Situational Dialogs

Dialog 1: *After receiving the products from Guangdong Falin Co. Ltd., Jenny found that some cartons were broken and the products leaked, so Jenny called Falin Company and lodged a claim.*

Jenny: Mr. Wang, I have to make a complaint to you.

Wang Lin: I am sorry to hear that. What's the matter?

Jenny: We regret to inform you that the goods shipped per S.S. "Shun" arrived in an unsatisfactory condition. 10 of the 50 cartons were broken and the products leaked.

Wang Lin: That's so unfortunate! How can that be?

Jenny: This is just what I want to ask and complain.

Wang Lin: I apologize for the inconvenience that has caused you. But each carton had been lined with foam plastics in order to protect the goods against press. Our way of packing has been widely accepted by other clients, and we have received no complaints whatsoever up to now.

Jenny: The fact is that some of the cartons were broken and the products leaked due to the poor packing. We are therefore compelled to claim against you to compensate us for the loss, i.e., USD 8,000 which we have sustained by the damage to the goods.

Wang Lin: I am sorry I can't entertain your claim. But I would keep my boss informed of your idea and get in touch with you once I get the solution.

Jenny: Thanks. This is the first time in many years that we have had to complain and we expect that you will look into the matter at once.

Wang Lin: Yes, of course. I will call my boss right now.

Dialog 2: *Guangdong Falin Co. Ltd. began to investigate the matter after receiving a complaint from Jenny. While apologizing to Jenny, Wang Lin sent the substitute products. At the same time, he promised Jenny to ship goods in stronger cartons.*

Wang Lin: Good morning, Jenny. This is the general manager of Guangdong Falin Co. Ltd. We are in receipt of your complaint and are sorry to note that the goods shipped per S.S. "Shun" arrived in an unsatisfactory condition. I heard 10 of the 50 cartons were broken and the products leaked.

Jenny: Thanks for your concern.

Wang Lin: We have made an investigation on the matter and found that we did make a mistake in packing.

Jenny: You can say that again. The damage was caused by improper packing.

Wang Lin: We apologize for causing you a good deal of inconvenience. As for the complaint, you asked a compensation of USD 8,000.

Jenny: Yes, what's your solution to this problem?

Wang Lin: You know, we have the same goods in stock. How about sending you the goods instead of cash compensation?

Jenny: That's acceptable.

Wang Lin: Thanks, we will make shipment immediately. We trust the goods will arrive in suitable time and be found to your satisfaction.

Jenny: I hope so. Please pay more attention to packing.

Wang Lin: Certainly. All the goods will be packed in stronger cartons. And we shall do everything we can to ensure that nothing like that will happen again and wish to assure you that extra care will be taken in the execution of your further orders.

Jenny: That would be fine.

Exercise

Work in pairs and make a business dialog with your partner on complaints and claims according to the information given in the cue cards.

Cue Card A

> You are Mr./Ms. Ye, the salesperson of an import company. You need to:
> - complain about the shortage of goods;
> - ask for compensation;
> - request to solve it immediately;
> - show thanks.

Cue Card B

> You are Mr./Ms. Broom, the salesperson of an export company. You need to:
> - apologize and promise to investigate into it;
> - agree to make compensation if it is the truth;
> - promise to solve it within one week;
> - expect good business relations.

Part ⑤ Skill Training

I. **Match the words and phrases in the left column with their translations in the right column.**

1. duly   A. 认定

2. take delivery   B. 清洁提单

3. consignment   C. 包装不良

4. insurance surveyor   D. 保险调查员

5. improper packing   E. 按时地；恰当地

6. sustain   F. 同意索赔

7. clean B/L   G. 调查

8. presume   H. 寄售货物

9. accept a claim   I. 经历，遭受

10. look into   J. 提取货物

II. **Fill in the blanks with appropriate words given in the box.**

as	in	shipped	regret
inform	attention	claim	

September 15th, 2022

Dear Sirs,

We have received your shipment covering our order No. 131 for 500 units of electric heaters, which you **1.** _____ by M/S "President", but much to our **2.** _____ we have to **3.** _____ you that one of the cases of your consignment is **4.** _____ a badly damaged condition. Among the goods, the panels of 42 heaters were broken and the mechanisms were exposed. It looks as if some heavy cargo had fallen on it.

5. _____ you see in our survey report stating 20 sets of heaters were severely damaged, these goods are quite unsalable. Therefore, we would ask you to ship replacements for the broken goods as soon as possible while we will lodge our 6. _____ with the insurance company. We hope the matter will come to your best 7. _____.

Yours faithfully,

Johnson Dong

III. **Choose the best answer to complete each of the following sentences.**

1. We reserve the right to claim compensation _____ you for any damage _____ the goods.

   A. with; to   B. from; on

   C. from; of   D. with; for

2. We have _____ the drums one by one and found that most of them are leaking.

   A. tested   B. roofed

   C. examined   D. rolled

3. Such being the case, we will hold the case _____.

   A. at your dispose   B. at your disposal

   C. for your dispose   D. for your disposal

4. We trust you will do your best _____ this matter settled at once.

   A. to have   B. to put

   C. to try   D. to be responsible for

5. _____ the matter, we found that a mistake was indeed made by us.

   A. On go into   B. On going into

   C. Upon go into   D. Upon going to

6. We are pleased to inform you that the item you requested can be supplied _____ stock.

   A. upon   B. out

    C. in   D. from

7. In view of the above, we cannot help _____ that you are complaining with the sole aim of obtaining from us.

    A. feel   B. to feel

    C. feeling   D. felt

8. In our last letter we sent you a copy of specimen contract _____ the usual sales terms and conditions.

    A. contains   B. contained

    C. being contained   D. containing

9. _____ S/C No. 7561, we opened the relative L/C yesterday.

    A. As regards to   B. With regard to

    C. Regarding to   D. Reference to

10. We'll make you an offer _____ receipt of your enquiry.

    A. as soon as   B. in

    C. at   D. upon

IV. Translate the following sentences into English or Chinese respectively.

1. 我会进行调查，尽快帮您改过来。

2. 您的客户账号输入我们仓库电脑时出错了。

3. 因重量短缺，买方对这批货物提出索赔 1 300 元人民币。

4. 关于你方产品质量低劣的问题，我方要求你方赔偿 15 000 美元。

5. 我们希望未来能为您提供良好的服务。

6. That shipment of parts from Japan has been partially lost and damaged at sea.

7. Unfortunately, when we opened this case, we found that the goods were short by five units.

8. The evidence you have provided is inadequate, therefore, we cannot consider your claim as requested.

9. We must prepare our claim and send it to the underwriter to secure payment.

10. This is the first time in all our transactions with you that some mistake has occurred, and we hope you will do your utmost to remedy it.

V. **Write a business letter according to the following situation.**

Guangzhou Yinyun Textile Company has reached an agreement of importing cotton prints from Canadian Sonny Company. After Yinyun Company had received the goods, they found the quality was far from being satisfactory. Please write a letter to Sonny Company to complain about the inferior quality of goods, covering the following points:

- complain about the quality, including rough workmanship, incorrect color;
- ask for compensation;
- request to investigate the matter and arrange shipment immediately.

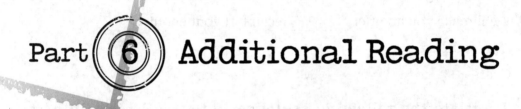

Part 6 Additional Reading

Settlement of Claims or Disputes in Foreign Trade

Complaints of Different Characters

It should not be necessary to complain. In ideal business conditions, everything should be done so carefully, with details of offers and orders checked, packing supervised, handling of goods carried out expertly that no mistakes are made and nothing is damaged. Unfortunately, as in other walks of life, nothing goes so well as that. Errors occur and goods are mishandled; accidents happen, usually because of hurry and lack of sufficient supervision. In certain matters, where it may be a question of fatal consequences, supervision must be and indeed is scrupulous, but in less vital matters this is not always so. There is often a shortage of staff owing to illness or holidays, sometimes a shortage of sufficiently trained staff, with resultant haste and overwork, so the mistakes creep in. All these, as a result, may lead to subsequent complaints of different characters. They may be:

- complaint of difference between goods delivered and goods ordered, or

- complaint of inferior quality, or
- complaint of missing or shortage from the delivery, or
- complaint of delay, or
- complaint of bad packing.

Handling Complaints with Great Care

We have seen that business relationships are largely a matter of contractual links between two parties: the customer being the buyer of goods or services, and the supplier being the seller of goods or the provider of services. All contractual arrangements must be mutually beneficial or business will cease. The buyer must receive goods or services of the kind or quality he anticipated; the seller must receive payment for goods or services. Failure to achieve either of these aims will lead to complaints. Making complaints is an unpleasant business and needs to be well-prepared and well-documented. Failure to make a complaint effective usually occurs as a result of inadequate presentation of the complaint. A vague complaint will almost always fail, for to give satisfaction over any complaint almost certainly reduces the profit, and if every vague grievance were to be compensated, business would become unprofitable and pointless.

Complaints should be made in a restrained and tactful way so that future business relationships are not jeopardized. A reference to an earlier course of business which has been untroubled and mutually beneficial will often lead to a more generous consideration of the complaint, and will arouse concern in the supplier for the preservation of the customer's goodwill. Claims should be requested firmly. Most reputable firms will propose an acceptable solution to the complaint, which may include some compensation for the trouble and inconvenience. Abusive language should never be used.